G8WAY

THE JOURNEY TOWARD YOUR AUTHENTIC SELF

David Blake · Domenic Thomas

Edited by Ned Sparrow

Cover & Graphics by Tom Desrosiers

ISBN-13: 978-0692327920
ISBN-10: 0692327924

Our Sincerest Thanks and Gratitude...

Becky, Nick and Meghan Blake
Jessica, Charlie and Jude Thomas
The Blake and Thomas families

The Alive Community(TAC)
David Blake Sr., Jeff Carstairs, Dan
Mastrocola, Stephanie Price, Sean Tumblety

Our generous co-contributors to this
book:
Tobias Bray
Tom Desrosiers
Ned Sparrow

To everyone who has touched our lives
over the years, with joy or pain and
everything in between. Thank you so much
for the lessons and love. We know you were
doing the best you could in every moment.

CONTENTS

THE G8WAY: OPENING THE G8WAY TO YOUR AUTHENTIC SELF

Introduction

This is a book about freedom. Freedom from the human condition as most of us have come to know it. The freedom to express your uniqueness authentically. To live your life according to your inner truth. To meet the joy and suffering of life as one. To embrace life as your own, in your own way, with clarity and compassion. The freedom to present ourselves, as we are in this moment, to the world. The freedom to feel *good enough* without any need for validation that does not originate in your own heart. To be a person who is a work in progress and not feel a single ounce of shame about it.

Everyone possesses the potential to live a life of authenticity.

The G8way is a framework to support your personal evolution towards greater physical, mental, and spiritual wellness. The G8way draws from our collective wisdom and the collective wisdom of humanity. We have designed the G8way to act as a guideline to support you in your journey of self-health. Our hope is it will become a living work, evolving as more people participate in it.

The G8way helps us discover who we are at a fundamental level. The process is one of moderation and being present with oneself. Letting go of ego and selfishness to reach a state of service to ourselves and everyone we

1

encounter in our lives. Service helps us find our authentic truth, our passion, our place in the world.

As you read through this book and apply the tools, you will discover your values and what beliefs support those values. Having these values in mind helps you to bring about actions and behaviors to align your life with your beliefs. The result is living a life of authenticity.

Know Thyself

We are all works in progress. Some might question this point, wondering what the goal is, or when we're supposed to arrive. The answer from our perspective is, we don't. We create a way of living which does not have an agenda. Sure, we have plans and direction, passion and purpose. Yet we don't allow these things to constrict our lives. We allow space for ourselves, for others, and for the world.

We pursue the freedom to live our birthright as human beings, as part of the collective whole of humanity and life on Earth. To cooperate with ourselves and everything which comes into our lives, in every moment. To live our purpose, our mission, to take our place in this world and share it with one another. To evolve and to change into whatever we were meant to be. No boundaries, no preconceived notions, no fear, just us.

Support

People need patience, faith and compassion to go through this process. We also need support to help us when we need it. The journey towards self-health may not be for everyone. Those recovering from severe trauma or other difficult health conditions must seek professional support. Our journey in life is our own. The inner work we do alone, but we are part of a greater whole and require the support of others to bring the best version of ourselves to the world.

Terms and Definitions We Use in This Book:

Self-health – Derived from self-help and preventative health, synergizing aspects of both at a holistic and integrated level.

Authenticity – Alignment of values and beliefs into action/habits.

Story – The consistent inner dialogue one uses to define the person they believe themselves to be. It is also the default "story" you tell others when they ask about who you are or what you do. When we begin to change our story, it becomes a narrative that promotes self-health.

Addiction – Addictions can include, but are not limited to, abuse of drugs, alcohol, sex, work, or food. An addiction can be any habit trading short-term pleasure for long-term negative effects.

Life of intention – Living according to our own internal value system. Intentional living is living beyond the influence of externals, neither being pushed nor pulled by external influences.

Self-audit – Taking, as objectively as possible, an inventory of who we are in any moment.

People-pleasing – Feeling the need to guide our actions primarily by how others will perceive us. Seeking others' pre-approval of our actions before acting.

Irrational thinking – Ineffective thinking which runs counter to our values and beliefs. Often influenced by negative emotional states.

Externals – People, places and things. Outside influences or environmental factors.

MAXIM 1 – POWERFUL CELEBRATION

powerful
1. Having great power or strength[1]

Once we recognize it is time for change we earn the freedom to reach out for assistance. People, organizations, and resources are available for us when we choose to ask for help. You're not permanently broken or done evolving! These bodies and minds given to us possess ALL of the necessary tools required to build and repair our lives.

I'm powerful!
-The Alive Community (TAC)-

Giving Away Our Power

self-doubt
a lack of faith or confidence in oneself.[2]

The self-doubt which often accompanies periods of stagnation can add much greater complexity to an already challenging situation. We begin to feel stuck, we neglect to care for ourselves, and finally the anxiety and fear begin.

This will begin to produce self-pity if it goes on long enough, and we begin questioning everything in our lives. Am I living up to expectations? Is this really the life I want to be living? These questions can have their place when they come from a position of authenticity and clarity. Sometimes it is worthwhile to perform a self-audit and really dig deeper into your own personal path and mission.

---

[1] https://www.google.com/search?q=powerful+deifinition&oq=powerful+d eifinition&aqs=chrome..69i57j0l5.3832j0j7&sourceid=chrome&espv=210&es_s m=122&ie=UTF-8

[2] http://www.thefreedictionary.com/self-doubt

> ### *The universe doesn't doubt you.*
> ### *-TAC-*

Self-doubt is a universal human experience, a place we have all visited at one time or another. It can be useful if it takes the form of self-inquiry or reflection. This is self-doubt without ego, judgment or comparing oneself to an external standard. We certainly do not believe we are always right and always possess the correct or perfect answer. In fact, this type of thinking is often a product of repressed feelings of self-doubt and low self-worth. However, if we can remain confident in ourselves while still being open to possibility, we gain a wider view of our lives. Some might view being uncertain as self-doubt, but we would suggest they do not occupy the same space: the first may wait for evidence and the second dreads and expects a bad outcome.

Self-doubt can also come from outside of ourselves. One of the ways we give away our power to others is through a need for external validation. When we have little faith in our inner voice we can feel the need to seek others' approval. This is similar to people-pleasing in that we want to feel that others not only like us, but they "approve" of our behavior or who we are. But there is no need to seek the approval of others to help us determine whether or not we are worthy. It is healthy to seek others' opinions at times, but know that your inner voice is more reliable.

The danger of self-doubt is its ability to lead us to self-pity. When we feel powerless, we can begin to feel sorry for ourselves. We can enter states of hopelessness and despair. We doubt whether or not a solution is even possible. We doubt our ability to make any meaningful change to our situation. These doubts can lead to externalizing our personal challenges or blaming the outside world for our unhappiness.

Negative self-talk can be a core aspect of perpetuating self-doubt and self-pity. We often consciously and unconsciously tell ourselves we are not good enough. We may even create boundaries to block our ability to improve or get well. We do the same for people, places and things in our lives. For example, anyone who tends to put a positive (optimistic) view on things might be seen as "fake" or "unrealistic." Is the person who believes everything is most likely going to go badly for them any more realistic than someone who believes it's more likely to go well? The mere thought of the word "change" presents possibility. At that single moment, the feeling of relief is available.

> *If you don't believe in change, do you believe in possibility?*
> *-TAC-*

People-Pleasing

Many of us go to great lengths to please the people in our lives. We have a desire to be liked. This is perfectly normal, except when we *NEED* to be liked. When we need to be liked by everyone in our lives, we create an impossible task for ourselves. We give away our power. This makes it very difficult for us to show any weaknesses or faults. We try to be perfect, to anticipate what will make others happy or what will make us most desirable to anyone and everyone we meet.

Neediness expects and generates rejection. When we compromise our own needs in order to please others, we reject ourselves. We are disappointed if the people we are trying to please do not seem happy or fulfilled by our actions. We feel rejected by others if we don't achieve our expected result. Rejection leaves us feeling powerless and disconnected. The truth is, we only enter a state of rejection when we compromise who we are. The true rejection is not in others' disapproval, but in the compromise of our authenticity.

One of the precious gifts we give away in our neediness is our authenticity. We no longer behave based upon what is right for us, our internal truth. Instead, we create an external image of what society or the people around us tell us is most desirable. We try to change who we are to fit the ideals sold by advertisements and pop icons. There are many attributes of this perfect person: physical attractiveness, material wealth, intelligence, relationship status, career choices. This ideal person no one can become is always available and eminently agreeable.

Depending on your culture or the people you are trying to please, there are thousands of other demanding attributes. Not all of these things are negative attributes. We need to find ways to compromise and cooperate with one another in order to form lasting bonds with each other. It's the way in which we pursue or project the "agreeable person" that causes us to feel alienated from ourselves. It's feeling "less than" when we don't possess some of these traits. Compromising our values and beliefs makes us feel like a fraud when we go out of our way to be something we are not. It's the judgment of ourselves and others, the inner and outer critic that makes us feel like we are acting or being auditioned.

> It is not the critic who counts; not the man who points
> out how the strong man stumbles, or where the doer of
> deeds could have done them better. The credit belongs to the
> man who is actually in the arena...
> -Theodore Roosevelt-

When we allow others' opinions to affect our self-worth, we give away our power. We have all experienced being the giver and receiver of judgment and criticism. Allowing this to shape us or change our behavior makes us feel powerless. We must understand that these things are a reflection of the person who engages in the judgment or criticism. They are rarely being objective or unbiased. If they were, it would be communicated with compassion and empathy.

Nine signs you are ready for change:

1. You're reading this.
2. You talk or complain about other people.
3. You consider yourself a procrastinator.
4. You're miserable and always the victim of circumstance.
5. You say aloud or in your head things like:
    - Everything was great and then of course, because it's me, these bad things happened.
    - I have horrible luck.
    - A black cloud always follows me.
    - People suck!
6. You're unhappy.
7. People refer to you as miserable.
8. You're afraid to live the life you dream about.
9. You're tired of trying to make everyone else happy.

What kinds of choices does your powerless self make? Do you make decisions based on what other people might think or what they want you to do? Do you behave in a manner to help soothe your self-pity? What are the results? How do these results reinforce your powerlessness?

How Does Our Powerless Self Take Control?

Every addictive act is preceded by a feeling of helplessness or powerlessness. The issues that precipitate these overwhelmed states of helplessness are unique to each person. Addictive behavior functions to repair this underlying feeling of helplessness. It is able to do this because taking the addictive action (or even deciding to take this action) creates a sense of being empowered – of regaining control – over one's emotional experience and one's life. Drugs are particularly good for this purpose because altering (thus temporarily controlling) one's emotional state is just what drugs do. However, non-drug addictions can be shown to work in exactly the same way, since addictive acts work to change (and therefore reassert power over) how one feels. The reversal of helplessness achieved by these addictive behaviors may be described as the psychological purpose of addiction.[3]

We often cope with feelings of powerlessness through addictive or compulsive behavior. These behaviors help us assert a sense of short-term power. To reiterate:

Addictions can include, but are not limited to, drug and alcohol abuse, risky activities centered on sex, gambling, work, or food, or any habits trading short-term pleasure for long-term negative effects.

The key here is "short-term": any activity that produces instant gratification does not create a sense of a powerful self at a fundamental level. These behaviors render us weak. Over time, they cannot be controlled and their ability to provide us with comfort diminishes. As we continue to engage in these behaviors, we feel even more hopeless and frustrated with our inability to take control of our lives.

Any time we feel powerless, we tend to feel anger. This can turn to rage and builds resentment. In Maxim 3 we discuss resentment as a fundamental barrier to growth. When we feel unable to express our true selves, we feel trapped and oppressed. The powerless self responds by taking control in any way it can. It engages in whatever means is available to bring about temporary control, often in the form of behaviors which are instantly gratifying. The

---

[3]http://www.psychologytoday.com/blog/the-heart-addiction/201010/the-psychology-addiction

powerless self rationalizes these choices without considering the long-term effects.]

Challenging Irrational Thoughts about Powerlessness

One of the ways we make ourselves powerless is with irrational thinking. Our internal chatter can render us powerless at any given moment. We are especially susceptible to irrational thinking when we are in a highly emotional state. One of the more effective techniques for dealing with irrational thinking is Cognitive Behavioral Therapy (CBT).

Cognitive-Behavioral Therapy is a form of psychotherapy that emphasizes the important role of thinking in how we feel and what we do.[4]

CBT recognizes thoughts as the basis for our feelings and behaviors. Many times when we are feeling powerless we believe we are a victim of our external environment. We believe we have no control in how we are affected by externals. A more rational perspective suggests we always have a choice. Events have an effect on us, but we decide how we feel about the event moving forward.

Neuroscience is beginning to confirm this concept by demonstrating areas of the brain that are stimulated by emotional triggers. These areas do create an initial, almost automatic, response. This response lasts for approximately ninety seconds.

Although there are certain limbic system (emotional) programs that can be triggered automatically, it takes less than ninety seconds for one of these programs to be triggered,

---

[4] http://www.nacbt.org/whatiscbt.htm

surge through our body, and then be completely flushed out of our bloodstream.[5]

So what do we do after the initial response? This is where CBT can help us develop effective ways to respond in a healthy and rational manner. CBT helps us uncover irrational beliefs we have in relation to the experience of our lives. We can counter these irrational beliefs by creating new beliefs to replace them.

For example:

Generally you say to yourself: (a) "I did this badly" and (b) "I therefore am an inadequate or bad person." You can change these beliefs to: (a) "Perhaps I really did act badly," (b) "Humans frequently do," (c) "Now let me, without any self-damning, discover exactly what I did badly and resolutely try to correct it next time."[6]

What we start to uncover as we go deeper with this concept is how to separate the action or behavior from the person. In Maxim 2, *Self Audit*, we will explain various methods of uncovering some of this irrational thinking without self-recrimination. We all make mistakes. We are not perfect. This doesn't mean we throw our hands up and do whatever we want regardless of the consequences. We can, however, avoid criticizing our core being simply because we have behaved poorly.

Reject the bad actions, not the actor.
-TAC-

We Always Have a Choice

If we want to live an intentional life, it is important to find the confidence in our ability to do so. This helps us

---

[5] "My Stroke of Insight" Taylor, p.153
[6] "A Guide to Rational Living" Ellis, Harper p.136

recognize we have the power to decide and create our future. We always have a choice. We may not like our options in any given moment, but we have a choice. If we take a closer look at the different aspects of our self, we notice our less powerful self makes different choices than our powerful self in any given situation.

We always have a choice. It might not feel that way sometimes, but once something happens, we decide what happens after. We might feel pain, sadness or frustration, but we don't have to feel hurt, depressed or angry. There is an opportunity in every moment to learn more about ourselves. We can decide whether or not an experience is awful or simply difficult, horrible or just uncomfortable. No one gave us a guarantee life would be easy. We decide whether or not we want it to be more difficult than it really is in any given moment.
I choose what I feel.
-TAC-

Vulnerability

When we are faced with great challenges, often we feel vulnerable and weak. Finding the inner strength to go forward and transform these challenges into opportunities requires internal power. Even when we feel weak, this power is something we all possess, at all times. Learning to summon this internal power in ourselves is crucial to our development. If we take some time to reflect on when we feel powerful and when we feel helpless, we will find there are some consistent behaviors associated with these feelings.

The key to our power lies in our vulnerability. Understanding that vulnerability is the building block of true strength takes courage. To live our lives with a truly open heart, without any secrets or façades, takes courage.

Vulnerability exposes us to the world. We feel uncertain because we are taking an emotional risk.

> *Vulnerability sounds like truth and feels like courage.*
> *Truth and courage aren't always comfortable, but they're*
> *never weakness.*[7]

One might say we face an even bigger risk by not allowing ourselves to be vulnerable. We rob ourselves of our own authenticity, of our right to feel a certain way or think a certain thought. By pretending to project strength and certainty at all times, we are acting, playing a role. This robs us of our feeling of self-worth because we create conflict among our values, beliefs and actions. To communicate our vulnerability is to stand up for ourselves. We can maintain healthy boundaries while still creating intimacy with others.

The essence of vulnerability is in not hiding any part of ourselves. We are allowing our authentic self to be available to everyone in our lives. It's a sense of openness to the world. We're not lying down; we're standing up for what we love and who we are.

Being vulnerable = truth. It is allowing us to present the best version of ourselves to the world. It creates space for other people in our lives to be who they truly are in our presence. This is powerful...This is courage...And it's contagious.

Aligning with Your Powerful Self

faith
1. confident belief in the truth, value, or trustworthiness of a person, idea, or thing.
2. belief that does not rest on logical proof or material evidence.
3. loyalty to a person or thing; allegiance.
4. a set of principles or beliefs.[8]

---

[7] "Daring Greatly" Brown p. 37

> *Inside all of us is an organic truth...an indicator of what aligns with us. Sometimes we refer to it as our Gut, God, Universe, Conscience, or Vibe, and it knows what is right and wrong for us. We all have it, but often we underutilize its ability to align us with what we need to be happy. We need to practice listening and following our own suggestions in order to live fulfilled lives. It's a gift. Don't deny yourself!*
> **Believe in your internal voice.**
> **-TAC-**

One of the defining characteristics of which part of us is showing up (powerful or powerless self) can be explained in terms of faith versus self-doubt. Our powerful self has faith in itself and the moment. The less powerful aspects we possess are often full of self-doubt. Believing in oneself is different than arrogance. Arrogance is self-centered confidence without the humility. Arrogance is full of judgment and belief that we are better or more important than other people. Faith believes we are good enough as we are. It implies a sense of humility and connection to the world around us.

> *To waken this inner artist, we must assume a certain shape that puts us in conversation with the elements; we must cultivate a kind of faith in the moving energies around us and the way they come to our aid, give us lift, no matter our circumstances or difficulties.*[9]

Faith is often considered to be a religious or spiritual concept, but faith is more than just a belief in something outside of ourselves. It is faith in who we are. Faith in where we are heading. It is a belief in our ability to persevere in

---

[8] http://www.thefreedictionary.com/faith
[9] *Crossing the Unknown Sea* David Whyte p.7

spite of life's challenges. Faith is belief in something in the absence of concrete proof or evidence. Faith is made up of feelings like confidence, self-worth and intuition. It is a fundamental component of wellbeing and positive self-worth. Many of us experience feelings of not being good enough. Developing faith in ourselves is important to help us realize we are all good enough. We may not be living a life of complete intention or authenticity, but we are good enough because we are here. It is the only qualification we need to belong to this world.

To believe your own thought, to believe what is true for you in your private heart is true for all men, — that is genius.[10]
-Ralph Waldo Emerson-

One of the foundations of engaging our powerful self is to have faith. Sometimes when we are feeling very weak and powerless, having faith in something outside ourselves is helpful. This might be the concept of higher power, religion, a group or even someone else in our lives that supports us. We might rely on this outer strength for a period of time while we connect to our inner strength and build our inner faith.

We then begin to develop faith in ourselves. As a result, we develop faith in the direction we are headed at any given time. This faith is organic. Over time it becomes faith in others and eventually faith in life. When we have a sense of purpose which is not dependent on a specific external factor, we have freedom. We gain strength and faith in ourselves through being of service to others. We offer our support without condition or motive.

---

[10] *The Works of Ralph Waldo Emerson - Self-Reliance* Ralph Waldo Emerson, p.97

Become selfless while supporting other individuals in their evolution. Asking for others to share the same support creates a power greater than ourselves. As a group we can reciprocate compassion, love, and support to empower each contributor with the strength they cannot replicate as an individual. Power in numbers is a stronger way to support transformation.

Power in support.
-TAC-

I'm Powerful

What do we mean by powerful?
1. The power to choose regardless of external circumstances
2. The inherent power of being human
3. The power to be of service to ourselves and others
4. Power without ego or judgment (humility)
5. Maintaining your authenticity
6. The ability to connect and contribute to the world

Sometimes, even when you love yourself
You're lonely
Even when you know who you are
And where you're going
You're a little lost
There is faith
But the suffering is great
Through the heartbreaks...we grow
With our hearts open
Opportunities
To expand our capacity for suffering
To remain fearless
Even without our skin to protect us
Or someone else to love us
-TAC-

It's Not What I'm Doing, It's What I Stopped Doing!

The distinct sudden change of realizing you have let go of something, even briefly, can be empowering. Success may not always be a measureable progress, but simply the act of shifting your space/paradigm to a new attitude or belief, a new consciousness. Letting go of behaviors or beliefs which no longer support our powerful self can be as important as the healthy things we bring into our lives. There may not be too many things we need to add. Sometimes it is more about what we discard or no longer identify with which can help our powerful self show up more often.

A great example of this is letting go of the idea that the world is conspiring against you. This is the concept of externalizing your discomfort or unhappiness. As human beings we often see what we want to see due to our own internal bias. If we believe the world is trying to do us harm, we will find confirmation of this throughout our daily lives. We are searching for things to confirm our beliefs. By letting go of this irrational belief, we suddenly find a new freedom, a friendlier world full of opportunity and resources to help us grow. As a result, we will begin to find confirmation of this new belief and begin to focus on the externals in our life for help.

Basic Goodness

Belief in your inner truth supports your powerful self. There has been much debate over the centuries as to the fundamental qualities of human nature. Philosophers have argued as to whether human beings possess a tendency toward being fundamentally negative, neutral or positive in their nature. What we are beginning to learn through the fields of neuroscience and psychology is, we are what we believe we are. If you choose to believe the essential nature of being human is good or positive, you begin to cultivate a sense of inner strength and belief in yourself.

> *When you don't punish or condemn yourself, when you relax more and appreciate your body and mind, you begin to contact the fundamental notion of basic goodness in yourself.[11]*
> *-Chogyam Trungpa-*

The concept of basic goodness can be traced to nearly all spiritual traditions and beliefs. Buddhism and most other spiritual traditions believe human beings are fundamentally good. It is in our nature to grow and evolve, to be of service to one another. We naturally flourish in situations where we cooperate with ourselves and others. By letting go of any negative beliefs about your inherent value or nature, you move toward a place of power.

Positive Reinforcement

In order to engage our powerful self on a regular basis it is important to develop exercises and tools to reinforce who we are and who we want to be. One of the exercises we can use is positive affirmations. Our language is very influential on ourselves and others. Our internal dialogue is sometimes filled with negativity and shaming language such as, "That was so stupid." "I have the worst luck." "I always make the wrong choices." This is the story we are telling ourselves and it reinforces our feelings of powerlessness. We can begin to change this inner dialogue by using positive statements about ourselves or by correcting these negative self-statements.

---

[11] "Shambhala – The Sacred Path of The Warrior" Trungpa, pp. 35-6

The essence of the conflict between traditional cognitive psychologists and psychotherapists is to engage in a process of analyzing your way out your problems, or the Third Wave approach which says, accept that you have negative beliefs, thinking and problems and focus on what you want. Third Wave Psychologists and coaches acknowledge that we have pain, but rather than trying to push it away, they say trying to push it away or deny it just gives it more energy and strength.[12]

Once we begin to correct some of these powerless statements, we can start the journey of affirming our powerful self. Positive affirmations help us see our strengths. We can begin by focusing on things we already believe are true about ourselves. Then we can progress to statements that reinforce the person we want to become.

The important part is to use statements in the present tense. Instead of saying "I will be," we use phrases that begin with "I am." It can be challenging to use positive affirmations at first if we really don't believe we are capable of the things we are saying, such as, "I am the most intelligent person in the world." It is more helpful to say, "I am pretty good at learning new things. I'm a quick study. I'm on it."

If we use positive affirmations continuously, we begin to change the way our minds perceive who we are and who we want to be. If we start by thinking about the traits of our powerful self, we can build upon and reinforce these traits over time.

Our verbal language is a powerful influence, but our body language may be even more powerful in the ways it influences how we feel and how others feel around us. Body language can have direct effects on our mood and behavior.

---

[12] http://www.psychologytoday.com/blog/wired-success/201305/do-self-affirmations-work-revisit

By simply changing our posture, we can change the way we feel and what we are communicating to others.

> *As it turns out, there is a simple method to both transform people psychologically and signal power to others: altering your body posture. Across species, body posture is often the primary representation of power. From fish to reptiles to lower mammals to human's closest evolutionary cousins, non-human primates, power is expressed and inferred through expansive postures, large body size, or even the mere perception of large body size through expansive postures.*[13]

Not only can our body language be used to help us feel more powerful, but it can improve our mood. Powerful postures help us feel in control and capable of action. The simple act of smiling is well documented as a way to improve mood. Even when we don't feel very powerful, a simple change of our posture can help us to align with our powerful self.

How Do We Support Our Powerful Self?

Daily Actions
*Physical * Mental * Spiritual*
*Eat * Read * Listen*
*Sleep * Meditate * Play*
*Exercise * Journal * Serve*

Maintaining a high level of health can be challenging without establishing fundamental habits to support one's body, mind and spirit. Most of us can find ways to cultivate ourselves here and there, but what does it take to create an ongoing practice to sustain our alignment and authenticity?

---

[13] http://www.scientificamerican.com/article/how-you-can-become-more-p/

Above we have outlined nine fundamental things we can do on a daily basis to support our health. The actions are broken down by their primary effect on our physical, mental and spiritual wellbeing. Nine actions might sound like a lot of work, but these things are simple to do on a daily basis. Establishing the conscious habit is likely to be the greater challenge for most of us. Here we will start with the physical actions. As we begin to live a life committed to growth, our physical health is a fundamental support system for this process. If we are tired and out of shape it will be especially challenging to find the discipline and motivation to continue working on our personal development.

Our physical health acts as a foundation for our mental and spiritual wellbeing. Our brain requires nutrition and rest in order to function at optimal levels. When we are working hard and challenging ourselves to grow, burnout looms.

Burnout can be as simple as feeling consistently over-stressed or overwhelmed to more serious physical conditions like adrenal fatigue or other severe hormonal imbalances. Burnout typically occurs when we experience high levels of stress combined with poor diet, lack of sleep, and/or little or no exercise. If we are to care for ourselves properly we must make our physical health a priority.

Daily Actions – Physical – Eat, Sleep, Exercise

1. **Eat** – Of course we need to eat, but we believe it goes beyond simply eating. Food is the primary nourishment of our bodies. If our diet is guided by sound nutritional principles, food becomes a tremendous aid in our growth and happiness on a daily basis. In addition, it is one of life's great joys.

2. *Sleep* – We all need sleep, of course, but do we get enough quality sleep to support a state of abundant energy? Sleep is essential to our body and mind's daily processing and repair mechanisms. Sleeping in a dark, clean, quiet and comfortable environment will support deep and restful sleep. Getting the proper amount of sleep is important, but without a deep restful quality, it will not support us in a healthy state.

3. *Exercise* – In the modern world, people survive with little or no exercise. This leads to a steady degradation of our health over time. We did not evolve as sedentary beings. Our bodies are designed to move on a daily basis and without exercise we begin to develop disease. Exercise is not optional if we are to remain in a healthy state. We need to combine a daily regimen of high and low-impact exercise to nourish our muscles, connective tissue and bones. Exercise is fundamental to mental health as well.

Exercise: Recognizing the Powerful and Powerless Self

Answer the following questions and include the following observations – body position, posture, facial expression and breathing – while answering.

Powerless Self

1. When do I feel self-doubting, angry, judgmental or fearful?
2. When am I people-pleasing at the expense of myself?
3. What kind of compulsive behavior do I engage in?
4. When do I feel weak or victimized?
5. When am I compromising my values and beliefs?
6. When do I engage in negative self-talk?

Powerful Self

1. When do I feel authentic, strong, loved, courageous, compassionate, and skillful?
2. Where does my internal power come from?
3. What do I have faith in?
4. What does my positive self-talk sound like?
5. When do I feel good enough?
6. When do I feel comfortable being vulnerable?

Tool: Body Language with Affirmation

Body Language: Assume powerful body positions daily.
1. Hands on hips, elbows out, feet spread.
2. Hands above head in V-shape, feet spread.
3. Chest out, chin up, shoulders back.

This is something you can use daily to start your day with a sense of power, or any time you are feeling powerless. It might be useful to do this before an important meeting or speaking event. Powerful body positions will help you to relax and improve confidence in any situation.

Positive affirmations: Positive affirmations can be combined every morning with power positions. Morning affirmations are straightforward and in the present tense. Start with no more than three or four. This helps to influence your subconscious and uproot sabotaging beliefs.

Examples:
I am powerful.
I have a choice.
I am grateful.

MAXIM 2 – SELF-AUDIT

It is easy to blame things outside of ourselves for our own unhappiness. We often wonder whether, if we could only control these things, everything would be great. Unfortunately this is like a cat chasing its tail. Happiness comes from within. Externalizing our emotions and projecting them onto events or people shifts the blame outward where it doesn't belong. Authenticity is a place of responsibility at all times. We decide what we want to bring into our lives, and how we perceive the experiences of our lives will determine future outcomes.
My emotions are driving my future.
-TAC-

How can we gain a rational and objective reference point for where we are right now? If you have the resources to seek the help of a coach or therapist, that's great and we encourage it. In this maxim we will go over ways to help you begin to find out who you are and what is driving your behavior right now. We start the G8way by finding our powerful self because you're going to want to go through the process of self-audit from this perspective. This process requires the authentic person within who can see things clearly and without being judgmental.

The most crucial aspect of the self-audit is to engage in this practice with pure honesty. If we cannot be honest with ourselves, we cannot get an accurate picture of who we are right now. Practicing honesty with ourselves also helps us to be honest with the people in our lives. It helps us to develop compassion for ourselves and others. Honesty is not easy. It can be one of the most courageous things we do in life, especially if we commit to being honest at all times.

We encourage you to go through this process from a place of self-compassion. Let go of feelings of shame, blame and guilt as they arise. Remember you are now doing something about the parts of you which cause pain and suffering to yourself and others. You are taking the time to put in the hard work and effort required to grow and evolve as a human being. This is the greatest gift we can give to ourselves and to others. In order to present the best version of ourselves to the world, we need to determine who is showing up right now, in every moment of our lives. From this point of clarity we can begin to choose which behaviors and ideas align with our powerful self and reduce those that do not.

Some of the questions we will be answering are:
1. What drives my powerless and powerful self?
2. What traits and characteristics do they possess?
3. What values and beliefs influence my actions?
4. What discourages my powerless and powerful self?

Where Am I?

Perspective

Finding clarity is a fundamental aspect of living a healthy and intentional life. When we are feeling hopeless or otherwise emotionally disturbed, it can be difficult to gain a rational perspective on our current situation. If we further engage in compulsive or destructive behavior, it can be even more difficult. We are caught up in our *story*. The story we consistently tell ourselves about why we do the things we do and what kind of person we are.

Often reality is different from our perceived truth about our current circumstances. Sometimes our powerful self runs the show. These are times when we look upon our actions as courageous, compassionate, or skillful. In these moments things feel right. At other times the parts of us that do not align with our authentic self are calling the shots. In these moments we often feel angry, judgmental or fearful. Our inner compass is off and we're upset in some way. We're powerless.

We possess an inner voice or intelligence that can calculate and describe our characteristics. We have the ability to view these characteristics and gauge the trait as positive or negative. By taking an honest and fearless inventory of our personality, thoughts, and character, we begin the process of building on our strengths and identifying weaknesses. This helps us to eliminate our less desirable habits at their core. Self-awareness is crucial to identifying our strengths and building our most respected self-image. Our values and beliefs are the most important indicators of who we are currently. Establishing our moral inventory, we can then begin to change, becoming who we want to be!

Find Your Story Part I

Nearly all of us have an underlying narrative or story we tell ourselves in every moment. It is not always at the forefront of our conscious mind. Sometimes it is our subconscious which is driving our behavior and thoughts. If we desire to live an intentional life, a life of choices as opposed to reactions, it is essential to find the content of our story. Here are some of the questions we need to answer:

1. What is the story I tell myself?
2. Is it accurate?
3. What is the story my powerful/powerless self tells me?
4. What do I believe?
5. What do I value?

6. What are my strengths/weaknesses?
7. Am I telling myself a false story because I am not truly honest?
8. Am I letting other people write my story?

Language

One of the primary ways we can determine some of the content of our story is through our language. Our internal self-talk and what we say to other people when we describe ourselves says a lot about the content of our story.

> *Be impeccable with your word...Through the word you express your creative power. It is through the word that you manifest everything. Regardless of what language you speak, your intent manifests through the word. What you dream, what you feel, and what you really are, will all be manifested through the word.* [14]
> ***-don Miguel Ruiz-***

Have you ever taken the time to observe your speech and think about what you are truly communicating to yourself and others? Language has a powerful influence on our thoughts and behaviors. It influences our emotional state and the people we communicate with. Many of us overstate its impact on others while underestimating the impact it has on us.

Verbal communication is a small portion of how we communicate with other people. Body language, context and emotional state play a much larger role in the message we send to other people. Internally, language plays a tremendous role in how we think and feel. Our internal dialogue influences our emotions, beliefs, and nearly all aspects of our behavior.

---

[14] *The Four Agreements,* don Miguel Ruiz pp 25-6

How Did I Get Here?

Recognizing Trauma

Recognizing the effects of traumatic events in our lives helps us to understand where we might need to engage in some emotional processing. Traumatic events can drive our behavior at a conscious and subconscious level. Understanding how trauma affects our behavior can help us become more self-aware. If the trauma has not been processed thoroughly or appropriately, we can take steps to help process it here and now.

"The only way out is through"

After we gain an understanding of how these past events affect our behavior, we can begin the process of looking into how we feel when this part of us surfaces in our daily lives. How do you feel when you are angry? Does the anger remind you of a past event in your life? When we have not processed an emotional experience in our lives completely, we carry the emotional impact of the event forward. If someone does something and we react with a feeling of anger, often we will bring the anger forward from prior events in our lives.

Unprocessed trauma is like an emotional debt we carry. It gathers interest similar to a financial debt, and the longer we live without processing it, the more it grows with greater intensity. If we have associated poor coping mechanisms with this past event, these mechanisms can be triggered when we feel similar feelings in the present. For example, if when you were a child you often felt unsafe, anything which makes you feel insecure in your adult life will trigger those feelings. If you used poor coping mechanisms like overeating or maybe substance abuse, you may feel a craving for these things when the feeling of being unsafe emerges as an adult.

An American poet, Robert Bly, has an excellent metaphor for how we carry unprocessed emotions or shame with us over the course of our lives. He uses the idea of a little black bag which we carry throughout our lives, and we place anything we don't like about ourselves or any shame we might experience in this bag. As we get older, the bag grows in size and we begin to forget it even exists.

This concept is based on the idea of a "human shadow" we all possess. The famed psychologist Carl Jung also wrote extensively on the subject. This little black bag weighs you down physically, mentally and spiritually unless you are able to find ways to "empty" the bag by processing these feelings and experiences in a healthy manner. With some practice, we can learn not to put any other shames and fears in the bag.

Conscious Beliefs

In order to effectively change our beliefs to support our values, we must find ways to discover these beliefs. When we find it difficult to enact change in our lives, we face a challenge and an opportunity. We need to pause and take a moment to think about what it is about this particular change that makes it so difficult. We often question our desire, commitment or will, when in fact it is likely that we are opposing one of our beliefs.

For example, if we are having a hard time changing our diet in order to lose weight, we need to explore our beliefs about food. If we believe we are depriving ourselves of pleasure when we stop eating unhealthy foods, this makes it very difficult to consistently eat in a healthy manner. Each time we make a choice to eat the healthy option as opposed to junk food, we are causing ourselves internal pain and conflict. If we change the belief from the idea of being deprived to focusing on the things we gain from healthy eating, we resolve this conflict.

Now every time we are faced with a food choice we think, "By making this choice I am moving closer to a healthier life." Eating junk food is seen as depriving yourself of a healthy lifestyle. Or put it this way: "This salt and sweet is going straight from my lips to my hips; I'll have a couple apples instead and improve my health."

What's Keeping Me Here?

Negative Self-Talk

> *A sense of worthlessness is created by your internal self-critical dialogue. It is self-degrading statements, such as "I'm no damn good,"…"I'm inferior to other people," and so on, that create and feed your feelings of despair and poor self-esteem."*[15]

Many of us will say things to ourselves that we would never tolerate if others said these same things about or to us. If a friend constantly told you the things you say and do are stupid or worthless, we would consider it abusive, yet we say these types of things to ourselves internally on a daily basis. We sometimes even say them out loud to ourselves after we make a mistake or make a poor decision.

We all make mistakes. Is it really "stupid" when we drop a pen? Or forget something inside the house on our way to work? It is far more rational to think of these things as simple common mistakes. Instead of "That was so stupid," how about "That wasn't the best idea/decision," or "Sometimes I don't make the best choices." These statements have a sense of self-compassion and forgiveness in them. They also reinforce that we don't "always" do stupid things.

---

[15] "Feeling Good," David Burns p.62

We can accept that we make mistakes and then take action to try and prevent them in the future without overanalyzing.

Perfectionism

perfection
: the state or condition of being perfect.
: the act of making something perfect or better : the act of perfecting something.
: something that cannot be improved : something that is perfect.[16]

You are perfect as you are! *-TAC-*

Perfectionism is an irrational ideal. It is a forever dangling carrot we chase in our minds. By definition, one can never attain perfection. One of the fundamental concepts of our existence is change. Nothing remains as it is from moment to moment. A rock may not change visibly in a millisecond, but physics tells us the atoms have moved. A microscopic piece of the rock has decayed. The same holds true for people. From the moment of conception, we are constantly changing. To achieve perfection we would have to freeze time, as any "perfection" we might attain is lost in the next moment.

No man ever steps in the same river twice, for it's not the same river and he's not the same man.
-Heraclitus-

What we typically mean when we say, "I'm a perfectionist," is we believe we give our best to everything we do, or we do not stop until something satisfies our

---

[16] http://www.merriam-webster.com/dictionary/perfection

definition of perfection. Alone this is not a negative character trait. The motivation to do our best helps us to evolve and reach our potential. As long as we do not believe we can arrive at a state of perfection and hold on to it, the motivation to improve is useful.

A conflict arises when we hold ourselves to an external standard of perfection, one dictated to us by society or other people in our lives, or even our perceived idea about what other people define as perfect. This is usually an unattainable standard for us and when we are unable to live up to this concept of perfection, we experience shame, low self-worth and other negative emotional states.

We are good enough just being ourselves and certainly have our hands full doing just that! It is not that we completely disregard other people in the world. This would be selfish and destructive. We need a certain amount of cooperation and conformity to form healthy social groups. However, when it comes to defining our own values and beliefs, our own ideals and our place in the world, we need not believe we are "no good" if we cannot live up to someone else's expectations.

Beliefs

belief

1. *something believed; an opinion or conviction: a belief that the earth is flat.*
2. *confidence in the truth or existence of something not immediately susceptible to rigorous proof a statement unworthy of belief.*
3. *confidence; faith; trust: a child's belief in his parents.*
4. *a religious tenet or tenets; religious creed or faith: the Christian belief.[17]*

---

[17] http://dictionary.reference.com/browse/belief

Beliefs are the perceived truths we hold. The way in which we "see" the world; our opinion of the way things are. Our beliefs are sometimes based on objective (factual) information. For example, the world is round, not flat. Our beliefs are often based on subjective (opinion) information, and learned from our parents, our religion, our experience, our education, our social groups and from society at large. Beliefs are the general ideas or concepts we base most of our decision-making on, in conjunction with our values. Our values drive us to act and our beliefs help us decide how to act.

Once accepted, our beliefs become unquestioned
commands to our nervous systems, and they have the
power to expand or destroy the possibilities of our present
and future.[18]
-Tony Robbins-

If you value people, you will generally find yourself seeking relationships with other people. If you believe people are generally "good," you might find most people to be pleasant and generally find yourself withholding judgment of them. If you believe people are mean, you are more likely to judge the people in your life more harshly, including yourself. Your actions will follow accordingly most of the time. In the case of someone who believes people are good, you will be more trusting and more compassionate. For those who believe people are mean, you will be skeptical of new people you might meet and less compassionate toward yourself and others.

It would take more effort to go against these beliefs in either situation. It takes conscious effort and self-control to go against your beliefs. As we discussed earlier, this requires more mental energy. As a result, we will only be able to

---

[18] *Awaken the Giant Within* Robbins, p.78

maintain this effort for a short period of time. So if you believe people are mean, you may be able to tolerate a crowd of strangers for a short period of time and appear friendly. But before too long, you will find yourself anxious to leave the situation or will become less engaging in conversation and social interaction.

Limiting beliefs are like blind spots: they hinder our ability to perceive things accurately. If we have a limiting belief, it reduces our ability to use our powerful self to help us achieve our goals. Limiting beliefs are almost exclusively associated with our powerless self. They are typically a reflection of the things we fear or an extension of our insecurities. If we look closely we will often find they are a result of the influence of external factors. They do not originate from our own internal truth. In order to find out where we might have a misalignment of our values and beliefs, it is important to understand that we have both conscious and subconscious beliefs.

I believed the lies
I believed I needed your acceptance
I believed I needed your love
I believed cynicism was a sign of intelligence
I believed sober people weren't having any fun
I believed substances provided answers
I believed I needed "things"
I believed the answers were out "there"
I believed in judging and being judged
I believed in fear
I believed in self-doubt
I believed in self-pity
It wasn't working out the way I thought it would or should or could
The lies almost killed me
I surrendered
I embraced change
I became comfortable being uncomfortable
I changed my "story"
I started listening to the voice inside

> *I aligned my values with my beliefs*
> *I took action*
> *I found my authenticity*
> *I turned into an Illusion*
> *I became "We"*
> **-TAC-**

Subconscious Influence

One of the hidden drivers of our behavior is our subconscious. This part of our mind often motivates us to act before we even realize it. It contains many of our past experiences that undergird and maintain our belief systems. If we were traumatized as children by our parents, we often have trouble depending on others and developing healthy intimate relationships as we mature. Our subconscious mind does not put a time stamp on these early childhood events.

If we are triggered by something in the present, we will begin to experience the emotions of a previously traumatic experience as if it is happening now. The triggering is automatic and can only be prevented in the future by processing the underlying emotion in a healthy manner. The triggering response may be reduced if we become consciously aware of the triggering events and how they relate to our past experiences.

"The stronger the unconscious influence, the harder we have to work consciously to overcome it. In particular this holds true for habitual behaviors. An alcoholic might come home in the evening and pour a drink; a person with a weight problem might reach for the potato chips--both easily casting aside the countervailing urge toward restraint."[19]

---

[19] January 2014, ScientificAmerican.com p.33

The difficulty in identifying our subconscious influences is that we cannot know them in advance of an event without practicing awareness. Until we are triggered, we are unaware of how the subconscious affects our thinking and behavior. By investigating our behavior through self-reflection, we can reverse-engineer the course that led to our actions. Once we identify a subconscious influence, it becomes much easier to recognize the impact on our behavior.

Bias

bias

a. A preference or an inclination, especially one that inhibits impartial judgment.
b. An unfair act or policy stemming from prejudice.[20]

Biases are an extension of our values and beliefs. We can almost say they are an intellectual product of our values and beliefs. Some biases are more universal to all human beings (negativity bias) while others are more unique to the individual, like a favorite color. Understanding how universal and individual biases affect our emotional state can promote greater self-awareness and understanding of what motivates our actions. Just knowing of and remembering a bias can help us exert more control over our actions and reactions. In many cases we can change or eliminate our biases if we desire to do so.

People generally look for others who agree with them. If you want to reinforce your values and beliefs, it is important to seek other people who hold views which align with you. If you want to change your attitude, then find people who represent your desired values and beliefs. In addition, you will be well served to find people who can compassionately

---

[20] http://www.thefreedictionary.com/bias

challenge you on occasion. This may help to reinforce your healthy values and beliefs, or open your mind to new perspectives and information.

Where Am I Going?

Asking for Support

We strive to maintain our own authenticity and to be accountable at all times for who we present to the world. This is mostly an individual process; only we can own it and take full responsibility for it. Along the way we often uncover things we need help with. We are not alone in this world. We all desire social connection and support. When we are unable to manage a situation on our own, it is important to identify when we need help. To seek the support of others is not copping out. It is just as wise to know when to ask for help as it is to know when we need to handle something alone.

Asking for help can be difficult, because we make ourselves vulnerable when we do this. We have learned in Maxim 1, *Powerful Celebration*, that vulnerability is strength. This may be true, but it doesn't feel strong when we ask for help. This learning to extend ourselves through connection with others helps us to form greater intimacy in our relationships. When we ask for help, we also provide an opportunity for others to be of service. A healthy, supportive relationship is one of give-and-take. Both parties gain something from the experience.

Uniqueness – Your Unique Gift?

Many of us have an interesting way of telling ourselves the right story at the wrong time. Believing in your own unique gifts is a healthy concept to be developed and helps to support our value in being of service to ourselves and others. Unfortunately, we use this concept of feeling as if we are the only ones who feel or are made a certain way when we are actually going through very common situations. A classic example of this is addiction.

When we are engaging in addictive or compulsive behavior, we often feel isolated. Of course, this is due to our anti-social behavior and unhealthy mental state, but we can begin to tell ourselves a story about how we are going through something no one else has gone through or is able to understand. Some of this develops during adolescence as we are beginning to learn how to relate to the world.

> *With these understandings of self-esteem and self-compassion during adolescence, we can see how personal fable and egocentrism plays a role in the development of these self concepts can greatly impact the way an adolescent views themselves and who they believe they are. If one is using personal fable to an extent that they constantly believe that nobody understands them, they are the only one who is going through "this" or they just feel alone all the time, this can very negatively affect their personal growth, self-esteem and self-compassion during adolescence.* [21]

This can lead us to believe that no one can help us, or that our compulsive behavior is really a part of our uniqueness. We will avoid the help and support of others because we feel they don't know what we are going through and can't possibly help us or give us proper guidance.

---

[21] http://en.wikipedia.org/wiki/Personal_fable

People in this state often go to great lengths to try and find complicated solutions to simple issues so they can perpetuate this myth about their isolation. This is often when people who are suffering will lash out if someone close to them attempts to help or bring them clarity.

The irony is that people often go through this in reverse when it comes to believing in their own authentic gifts and talents. The same person who above is caught up in compulsive behavior, convinced they are alone and unique in their situation, will then tell you they are just like everyone else when it comes to any skills or talents they might possess. They may have a calling for the arts or the desire to start a business, yet they will tell you they don't possess the unique qualities they believe are necessary to do so. This is often the time when believing in your uniqueness is the authentic and truthful choice.

Values

value

1. the regard that something is held to deserve; the importance, worth, or usefulness of something.
2. a person's principles or standards of behavior; one's judgment of what is important in life.[22]

Values are the foundational aspect of who we are and who we aspire to be. The things we hold most dear and which are most important to us are our values. They may change to some degree over time, but they are fairly consistent throughout our lives. Virtues are aspects of humanity we universally hold to be of the highest moral

---

[22]https://www.google.com/search?q=what+are+values%3F&oq=what+are +values%3F&aqs=chrome..69i57j0l5.2559j0j7&sourceid=chrome&espv=210& es_sm=122&ie=UTF-8

character. They are things we regard as the best part of our collective humanity.

...we read Aristotle and Plato, Aquinas and Augustine, the Old Testament and the Talmud, Confucius, Buddha, Lao-Tzu, Bushido (the samurai code), the Koran, Benjamin Franklin, and the Upanishads–some two hundred virtue catalogues in all. To our surprise, almost every single one of these traditions flung across three thousand years and the entire face of the earth endorsed six virtues:

- *Wisdom and knowledge*
- *Courage*
- *Love and humanity*
- *Justice*
- *Temperance*
- *Spirituality and transcendence* [23]

Values are often directly related to human virtue. Many people value their family and friends, which is an extension of the virtue of love and humanity. We might simplify this value as "relationships." The most important thing is to understand how values drive our behavior, and how they influence who we are and who we aspire to be. Values are the core aspects of self. Values give our lives meaning. They influence nearly all of the decisions in our lives.

Values are supported by our beliefs about them. If we do not have alignment of our values and beliefs, it is very difficult to engage in appropriate actions and behaviors. One of the most difficult tasks we face is trying to make good decisions and take proper action in our lives when our values and beliefs are not aligned.

Values and beliefs are not rigid concepts we use to bully our way through the world. It is important for us to maintain our authenticity, but it can be easy to become arrogant and demanding if we are not flexible in terms of

---

[23] "Authentic Happiness" Seligman, pp. 132-33

43

how we put them into action. We do not need to compromise our values and beliefs, but we might find it useful to simply vacate a situation that doesn't align with us as opposed to forcing our values and beliefs onto others.

Unconditional Self-Acceptance

One irrational belief that undermines our ability to achieve a healthy state of self-worth or self-esteem is our dependence on what other people think of us. We compare ourselves to an impossible external standard to determine our value. The underlying issue with this is other people's opinions are constantly changing toward us. Ultimately, they do not have the ability to provide us with self-worth.

> *No matter how much others approve of you, or how much they may value you for their own benefit, they can only give you...extrinsic value, or worth to them. They cannot, by loving you, give you intrinsic value – or self-worth.*[24]

To recognize the futility of extrinsic validation is the essence of identifying with your own inner power. YOU decide your own value to this world and to everyone in it. This is your choice and it cannot be taken away from you unless you allow it. Aligning with your powerful self doesn't mean you'll always feel perfect or even powerful. Sometimes you will feel vulnerable or weak. The difference is, when you feel those things, it will not make you feel less valuable as a person. You connect with the power in feeling every aspect of who you are and understanding your power is derived from being you...nothing else. This authenticity is the baseline of your self-worth...your self-esteem...your value to yourself and others.

---

[24] *A Guide to Rational Living* Ellis, p.11

Signature Strengths

Signature strengths reflect core positive character traits we naturally possess as individuals. They are often associated with general human virtues. These traits represent aspects of our self which we can rely on consistently to lead successful and fulfilling lives. They can certainly be developed over time and improved upon, yet when we engage in situations where these strengths are favored, we find ourselves performing well almost effortlessly.

We encourage you to contemplate parts of yourself which you believe are your natural strengths or talents. Make a list of some of these and compare them to your core values. Discovering these strengths will help you to align your unique gifts with your personal mission. In Maxim 6, *Dream Design and Visualization*, we will further expand on finding your mission or soul purpose.

Values + Beliefs + Actions = Authenticity

Happiness is when what you think, what you say, and what you do are in harmony.
-Mahatma Gandhi-

When we have made progress by establishing healthy behavioral patterns, we often see an alignment which supports this behavior. If we have established a healthy sleep pattern, for example, we will find alignment of a value (personal health and wellbeing), a belief (sleeping is fundamental to good health) and an action (regular, healthy sleeping pattern). Because we have reduced our internal resistance to the improved behavior, getting better sleep is easier. The wonderful thing about this action is its authenticity: it comes from inside us; it is not imposed on us by any externals. We are not engaging in this behavior because we "should" or because it will make someone else happy or because someone told us to do it. We are doing it because it aligns with our core value system and we have healthy beliefs supporting this value.

This is something we work on over the course of our lives. We don't beat ourselves up because we are unable to achieve full alignment of our values, beliefs and actions. This is one of the essential aspects of being a work in progress. The key is to use our self-awareness and the tools we have to take a look inward when we find ourselves behaving in an undesirable manner. We have learned to get underneath the behavior by going deeper and withholding judgment. When we do this, we can take an honest look at what motivated us to act: Was it greed? Need? Addiction? An effort to please a faraway parent? We'll know better next time because of our practice.

By granting ourselves this compassionate approach to our growth and development, we are then able to extend this to others. We no longer quickly judge another person's behavior without putting ourselves in their shoes. We are more capable of empathizing with their situation, because we are aware of our own process. We can see a part of ourselves in everyone we meet, in all of our relationships, including the relationship we have with ourselves.

We possess the ability at any moment to align ourselves with our core values. We don't have to think of a way to change the world, come up with the next Facebook, or invent the alternative to the iPhone. We can keep it simple and eliminate all the unnecessary chatter and distraction. When we are true to ourselves by aligning with our internal values and beliefs, we get what we need. It seems too simple to be true, but it is! Many times when everything is good in our lives, temptation appears. By resisting the desire to indulge and therefore avoiding destructive behavior, we send out a higher level of vibration. The law of attraction unites our like-minded standards and we receive similar greatness. Your soul is your tool.

> *Aligning with my core values is a daily opportunity.*
> *-TAC-*

Exercise: Experience Clarity

Objective: Experience a level of clarity that will serve as a reference point.

This is an opportunity to allow your mind, body and spirit the experience of complete clarity. By dedicating our energy to an uninfluenced or unmanipulated mind, body, and soul, we engage our organic self. The reward of this exercise is an opportunity for transformation.

1. Make a list of all of the things that you do now that fit into the category of addiction: food, alcohol, pornographic material, drugs, social media, sugar, fat, smoking, etc.

2. Make a commitment to abstain from these behaviors.

3. Share your commitment with the people around you that will support you.

4. Identify and avoid triggers that will challenge you. Be mindful of environment, places, people, things – the externals that may not align with this exercise.

5. Track your progress by marking the day you started.

6. Commit to this exercise for four weeks.

This is the exercise for you if these thoughts are in your mind:

I can stop any time I want to.
It's not a big deal so it's not a big deal.
I always wanted a reason to try this out.

Tool: View Your Language

Our language can tell us so much about our internal state. It reflects our conscious and subconscious beliefs. Language has a heavy influence on our emotional state as well. Throughout the day, observe when you use harsh or negative language.

1. When you are upset, do you use words like horrible, terrible or awful?
2. Do you call yourself names?
3. When you are speaking about certain people does your tone and language change?
4. Do you often complain about externals?
5. How often do you say could, should and would? Or can't, never and always?
6. How often do you use curse words?

MAXIM 3 - RESENTMENT AT PEACE

resentment
Indignation or ill will felt as a result of a real or imagined grievance.[25]

The biggest resentment of all is holding on to the resentment.
-Dan Mastrocola-
-TAC-

Identifying Resentment

When we find ourselves wanting to process an emotion, we need to give it a voice. We can write about it, speak about it, draw it, whatever helps us to express the emotion outwardly. Emotions that are internalized are the ones that typically cause us long-term discomfort and dysfunction. We are unaware of how they affect our everyday life and behavior. Once we begin to bring these internalized emotions out, we can then process them in a healthy manner.

Resentment is an emotion we are often unaware of consciously. We may not even be able to identify most of the resentments we hold until we start looking for them. It takes practice, but over time we become able to recognize resentments the moment they begin to form. We no longer need to hold on to them and we can give them a voice immediately and let go of the resentment.

One of the best ways to identify resentment is to write out a resentment list. Think of externals in your life that you blame for past and present misfortunes. Is it someone else's

---

[25] http://www.thefreedictionary.com/resentment

fault you are unhappy? Then there is probably a resentment you hold toward them. Is someone or something holding you back from living the life you want to live? There's resentment in there. If you get angry when you talk about a particular person or event, you are likely holding on to resentment.

Ask yourself some of these questions and write down any resentment you find. Talk to someone close to you that you trust and ask them if they notice any time you seem resentful. Once you have a list of resentments, you have begun the process of giving your resentments a voice.

Find Your Story Part II

In Maxim 2, *Self-Audit* we introduce the concept of our story. This is our self-identity narrative, a story we tell ourselves every day. Different parts of our story reflect different aspects of the person we believe we are. The person we believe we can and can't be. The story of ourselves is born from our values and beliefs and has ultimate influence on our behavior. If resentment is a common thread in your story, you are bound by it indefinitely. Unacknowledged resentments are like emotional straightjackets: they trap us into feeling powerless. When we make resentment part of our story, we create obstacles to our growth and development.

Ask yourself these questions:
1. Do you find your story is full of people, places and things you hate or despise?
2. Are there parts of you which you cannot bear to admit to or accept?
3. Do you have the right to be angry about someone or something?

If you are answering yes to any of the above, you have made those resentments a part of your identity. You have given these events great influence over how you feel and how you behave. Some people call this "renting space in your head" or being "owned." We become a prisoner to these storylines as we let them define who we are. They determine our self-worth. By holding on to them we often magnify the impact of the initial experience. Over time, our version of the event becomes more painful than the initial event.

When we make resentment part of our story, we are identifying with being a victim. This makes us feel more and more powerless over time. There are things people do to us which are painful, traumatic and sometimes catastrophic. However, we decide what happens after the initial event. We can distance ourselves from the external event and take steps to prevent it from occurring again, but we have a choice as to whether or not we want to relive the event over and over again.

Resentment sometimes cripples us. Externals only own us when we grant permission. If we allow a resentment to live within us it only builds momentum, steals energy, and derails our true purpose. We are a victim when resentment runs the show. We forfeit our happiness and freedom when resentment resides in our heart or mind. Deciding who is right or wrong, waiting for an apology and energizing anger are reactive emotions. We can turn this around by changing our perception, and respond by taking control through powerful action. Success is a frame of mind. When we allow our powerful mind to show up and take control, we realize the strength is in forgiveness. Don't give your happiness and energy away. Asking for forgiveness comes from strong character. Respect yourself enough to move on from the things that don't deserve your energy.
Let them be correct and you will be free!
- TAC-

Justified Anger

...But the guy was a complete and utter dick!
-Anonymous-

One of the more challenging aspects of letting go of resentment is when we feel we have the right to be angry. We certainly have the right to feel any emotion when something is happening to us or to someone we care for. But just because someone did something we perceive as wrong or hurtful does not mean we have the right to be angry about it for the rest of our lives. In fact, we are often more indignant about resentments which we feel are justified because we see a part of ourselves in it that we don't like.

If we can take some time to put ourselves in the other person's shoes for even a minute, we can begin to see nothing is entirely right or wrong. This type of black-and-white thinking often leads us to suffering. If you can take the time to sit down and think about why the person might have behaved in the manner in which they did, you can often see some reasons which are not entirely evil or premeditated. When people lash out at others, it is almost never personal. They didn't stop and think, "I am going to absolutely ruin this person's life for no reason except to watch them suffer." Their intention may have been negative or malicious in its purpose, yet even in this rare instance, their anger is still not about us.

Every human being has lashed out at someone out of their own emotional pain at some point in their lives. We are not above or below the behavior of others. When we try to separate ourselves from other people, it is often because we are judging them and, conversely, judging ourselves.

People are doing the best they can in any given moment.
-TAC-

It may not be a great effort and it might hurt others, but in that moment they have made a choice and they believe it is the best choice at that time. It is a product of their emotional state, their own story and the environment or situation they find themselves in, as well as their relationship to it. Holding resentment toward someone is a type of ultimate judgment, where we have nominated ourselves as both judge and jury.

Resentment and Bias

bias
Bias is an inclination of temperament or outlook to present or hold a partial perspective, often accompanied by a refusal to even consider the possible merits of alternative points of view.[26]

Resentment can grow easily out of bias. To some degree we all hold on to various biases. We might be prejudiced toward certain people or cultures. We may be biased toward certain types of people; for example, those who appear smart, beautiful, or athletic. There are dozens of different biases found in human behavioral patterns. The more aware we are of those biases that affect our perception, the less impact they have on our thoughts and behaviors. Biases are far more powerful when they are unknown to us.

One of the more powerful biases in terms of resentment is the negativity bias. Some researchers believe this is a universal bias shared by all human beings. There are different aspects to the negativity bias involving how humans react to and perceive various negative events or objects. In terms of our emotional state, the negativity bias affects us by putting more value on the negative parts of an experience than the positive. When we bear negative

---

[26] http://en.wikipedia.org/wiki/Bias

consequences for our actions, we may initially focus on the pain or suffering of our punishment without seeing the value in the lesson we learned in the process. For example, we didn't beat ourselves up about how dumb hot stoves are the first time we got burned. We cried and learned. "Who left the burner on? Why does this always happen to me?"

A negativity bias can become an ongoing resentment toward the world. We become focused on things that are not working or externals that reinforce our bias that life sucks or that things never work out for us. Bias is a way we select information in our daily lives. As humans we have tremendous processing power, but we cannot possibly process every bit of information we come across throughout our day. Bias is an important psychological filter. Bias helps us to select crucial information. We filter for what we think is most useful for us, but in fact sometimes what we perceive as useful may harm us.

Externalizing/Awfulizing

Sometimes we feel like the world is conspiring against us. We take it all personally. We believe we are unhappy because the external world is unfair, especially when it comes to us. Other people are lucky and fortunate; we are cursed. Such catastrophizing is one of the most destructive perspectives we can take in any given situation. We immediately render ourselves powerless ("There's nothing I can do; everything is against me"). We quickly move to self-pity and inevitably to resentment. We resent the people in our lives because we perceive they have gone out of their way to cause our suffering. We resent the world because it is unfairly and unjustly targeting us.

Self-centeredness props up such a worldview. We believe the world revolves around us while simultaneously feeling as if we are totally inadequate, a very dangerous psychological combination. As long as we believe we are being unduly persecuted, it will undermine our ability to gain a rational perspective on our lives. This belief colors nearly everything we do from day to day. We are constantly scanning for evidence to back up this belief and essentially creating a negativity bias on steroids.

When someone does something which creates an emotional reaction in us, we have a tendency to take it personally and we abandon our responsibility in the matter. We take away our ability to choose how we react to the situation and engage our habitual emotional response patterns.

> *Your seeing any unfortunate Activating Experience or Adversity as **awful, horrible, terrible** deludes you that you absolutely **cannot** cope with the **awful** essence of the universe that plagues .... No matter how **unfortunate** or **undesirable** an event is, you still are able to cope with it. But if you see it as truly **terrible**, you surrender almost all control you may have over it (and over your feelings about it), and you subject yourself to worse misfortune.*[27]

Such demonizing presents a way for us to avoid dealing with emotional pain and suffering. We seek distraction and escape out of habit. It becomes much easier to do this when we feel "justified." If we can lay the blame for our feelings and emotions on someone or something outside of ourselves, we no longer need to accept the responsibility for our part in it. We may feel relief in the short term, but over time we have given away our power and put our powerless self in charge. This creates a cycling effect where we begin to consistently find confirmation that the world is out to get us and we have no chance of finding clarity in our lives.

---

[27] "A Guide to Rational Living" Ellis, Harper p.90

Shame

*Shame is the intensely painful feeling or experience of
believing we are flawed and therefore unworthy of acceptance
and belonging.*[28]

Shame is isolating. When we feel shame, we feel as if we
are the only person in the world who feels this way. We feel
unworthy and disconnected from others. Shame is one of the
strongest emotions and renders us powerless. Shame
summons self-pity and/or self-loathing. As a result, shame
activates resentment.

When we feel shame as a result of someone else's
behavior, we often feel *ashamed* of our reaction or our
inability to prevent the event from happening in the first
place. This is part of feeling victimized. If we hold on to the
resentment, we feel shame because we can't let go of the
event. We know in our hearts holding on to the resentment
is unhealthy, yet we can't seem to let it go. Many times
shame glues the event or person in our conscience.

Shame is not the same as guilt. Guilt is a feeling of
knowing we have violated our personal values and/or
beliefs. We didn't act in alignment with our authenticity and
we are sorry for it. Shame is based around the phrase "I am
bad" while guilt revolves around the knowledge "I did
something bad." When we feel shame, we are rejecting
ourselves; when we shame others, we are rejecting them.
When we feel guilt, we are rejecting the behavior only.

Eliminating Self-Resentment

*Starting over is overrated! At times it may seem as if it is the only
solution due to pain, embarrassment, or avoidance of repercussions.
Maybe it feels as if everything to this point was for naught:*

---

[28] "I Thought It Was Just Me (But It Isn't)" Brown p.5

> *All the hard work in the past, along with the dedication, has brought you back to that place you never wanted to feel again. How did this happen again? Why didn't I learn my lesson? Well, isn't the lesson in the mistake or the failure? If not for the suffering, we would have nothing to gauge the happiness. Every experience is a piece of our journey defining our character. Starting over would remove so many lessons of life that have shown us what we believe in and who we want to be. We are a work in progress and every step brings us closer to our own identity.*
> **My past carved me for brilliance.**
> -TAC-

Resentment starts with us. Any grudge we hold against an external is often a reflection of some part of ourselves we don't like, something we are ashamed of or judge in our own character. Human beings rarely find a deep emotional connection to anything they don't relate to. We have a hard time forgiving and letting go of our anger if we cannot give ourselves a break. We are often our own harshest critic. Our irrational expectations lead us to try to be perfect.

When we find we are holding on to resentment, the first place to look is inside. What part of us do we see in the resentment? Have we done something like this to someone else before? Did this person engage in behavior that reflects a part of our own character that we reject? Are we blaming or judging this person for another event that happened in our lives?

Self-resentment starts with phrases like, "I can never forgive myself for…" "What I did was unforgiveable…" and "I'll never get over…" It is often based around things we wish we could take back or do over – things we are ashamed of. So we continue to punish ourselves internally as if this will lead to some sort of redemption. The reality is, we cannot undo things or take them back. They happened. We are not perfect. We make mistakes. In this moment we can only learn from them and take the necessary steps to prevent unseemly behavior in the future.

Eliminating Resentment of Externals

Strangely enough, we blame others and put so much energy into the object of anger or whatever it is because we're afraid that this anger or sorrow or loneliness is going to last forever. Therefore, instead of relating directly with the sorrow or the loneliness or the anger, we think that the way to end it is to blame it on somebody else. We might just talk to ourselves about them, or we might actually hit them or fire them or yell. Whether we're using our body, mind – or all three – whatever we might do, we think, curiously enough, that this will make the pain go away. Instead, acting it out is what makes it last.

*"Drive all blames into one" is saying, instead of always blaming the other, **own** the feeling of blame, **own** the anger, **own** the loneliness, and make friends with it.[29]*
-Pema Chodron-

Our resentment toward externals is an extension of our externalizing behavior. We may not feel comfortable accepting our part in it. We may not want to face the emotion that may have been triggered by the event. In many cases we think to find relief by blaming someone or something and thus reduce our own pain and discomfort.

Authenticity is total accountability at all times. We don't have the luxury of discarding our accountability when it's convenient. If we can find the courage and patience to simply feel the pain or discomfort, we are able to process the emotion in a healthy manner. This allows us to let go, avoiding resentment in the first place. It further allows us to see the world as a supportive place, rather than one undermining our happiness. Our relationship to externals dictates how they affect us, not the other way around.

---

[29] "Start Where You Are" Chodron p.53

Our powerful self may see these things as an opportunity to grow, to develop, or to find a solution. Through blaming we often want to project our pain outward in an attempt to relieve our discomfort. This is another example of short-term gratification in exchange for longer-term suffering. Lashing out extends the cycle and further causes harm to others. If we can learn to simply sit with things, sometimes we may find these externals are not as harmful as we once believed. We can attempt to sit between holding on or running away or acting indifferent. There is a clear, present and insightful space between these three behaviors.

Compassion

compassion
sympathetic consciousness of others' distress together with a desire to alleviate it.[30]

Compassion is the antidote to anger. It is the most powerful and complete way to resolve lingering resentment. When we can see resentment from the perspective of our powerful self, we can empathize with the external we have been holding resentment against. We can have compassion for the person who made us angry or caused us pain. We can relate to the pain, frustration, fear or anxiety they may have been feeling in that moment. We can also have compassion for ourselves.

We understand why we were upset and why we held on to the pain and suffering for so long. This is the beginning of healing. This is the process of allowing ourselves to feel the emotion and allow it to run its course once and for all. When dealing with emotions, most of our suffering comes after the initial event as we choose to avoid the emotional pain and

---

[30] http://www.merriam-webster.com/dictionary/compassion

trauma, rather than being present with it and allowing it to pass through us. Resentment is an extreme version of avoiding the initial pain and bottling it up for later.

Compassion is critical to intimacy. Without it we have no way to empathize with others. If we can only see them through the lens of judgment or utility (what they can do for us), we miss the beauty of their flaws and the reflection of our own flaws. Without compassion we have a hard time understanding other people's motives because we can only see their actions through the effect on us. We become critical of their behavior whenever it doesn't serve our agenda. We take everything personally because we cannot connect to others. In condemning others in this way, we ultimately condemn ourselves.

The only way out is through
The emotion lies hidden underneath
At once long forgotten,
But always remembered
Until you find yourself
Somewhere, down below,
The conscious veneer of the mind, body and soul
Attachment and craving show you the way
Everything is the path
Yet nothing is clear
Faith
Perseverance
Patience
These three are my guides
These three truths.
-TAC-

Self-Compassion

To begin developing a more compassionate attitude, we start with ourselves. If we are unable to practice compassion toward ourselves, it is very difficult to practice it toward others. When we do not show ourselves kindness and forgiveness, we reinforce feelings of shame or unworthiness. This makes it very difficult for us to find the mental space to extend compassion toward others. Most of what we think and feel about ourselves is what we will project onto other people. A critical, blaming attitude toward ourselves will lead to similar treatment of others.

Self-compassion is the beginning of clearing any resentment we hold toward our own past behavior. Self-resentment is a part of our story. We see ourselves as being worthy of resentment and therefore find others worthy of it as well. If we can forgive ourselves and practice some understanding and empathy toward ourselves, we can begin to let go of all resentments.

Part of our internal resentments can come from feeling as if we didn't stand up for ourselves or protect ourselves properly when the initial event occurred. Here again we are blaming, except we are blaming ourselves for feeling pain and suffering! **Self-compassion recognizes we also did the best we could in that moment.** We may want to do things differently in the future, but we can have compassion for the part of us that was hurt in that moment.

Self-compassion involves acting the same way towards yourself when you are having a difficult time, fail, or notice something you don't like about yourself. Instead of just ignoring your pain with a "stiff upper lip" mentality, you stop to tell yourself "this is really difficult right now," how can I comfort and care for myself in this moment? Instead of mercilessly judging and criticizing yourself for various inadequacies or shortcomings, self-compassion means you are kind and understanding when confronted with personal failings – after all, who ever said you

61

were supposed to be perfect? You may try to change in ways that allow you to be more healthy and happy, but this is done because you care about yourself, not because you are worthless or unacceptable as you are. Perhaps most importantly, having compassion for yourself means that you honor and accept your humanness. Things will not always go the way you want them to. You will encounter frustrations, losses will occur, you will make mistakes, bump up against your limitations, fall short of your ideals. This is the human condition, a reality shared by all of us. The more you open your heart to this reality instead of constantly fighting against it, the more you will be able to feel compassion for yourself and all your fellow humans in the experience of life.[31]
-Kristin Neff-

Compassion for Others

The process of embracing past resentments is one of the most effective actions in self-development. Our past experiences with externals can limit our spiritual growth. When we look back at times of pain, shame, and fear from a place of power we can see the lessons and character development we received. The negatives we hold onto sap our will and evolution. No good comes from allowing the past to live in our future.
The power is in forgiveness.
-TAC-

To let go of resentment, we eventually must find a place of compassion for the target of our resentment. If we cannot find a way to connect ourselves to the person who hurt us, we cannot heal the resentment fully. Healing a memory of hurting requires a deep understanding of the entirety of the situation. We build a new relationship to the external by focusing on understanding and connecting to it. The core component is empathizing with the external you resent. It is

[31] http://www.self-compassion.org/what-is-self-compassion/definition-of-self-compassion.html

typically easier to have some compassion for ourselves when we feel we have been wronged or hurt. It can be very difficult to find compassion for the person we believe wronged us.

Practicing compassion takes time. It is a skill we can acquire with practice. It is not only available for those things we consider good. Compassion is inclusive and when it is fully realized it is available for everyone and everything in our lives. Not just the people we like, but compassion for those who harm us. Practicing compassion requires us to let go of judgments and biases. We are asking ourselves to relate to the situation intimately. This further allows us to build intimacy with ourselves, even a part of us that was wounded and hidden. When we spend our lives rejecting things, we isolate ourselves. Unfortunately, this also reduces our ability to relate to those things we find to be useful or desirable in our lives.

Exercise: Resentment List

Write out a list of resentments you are holding on to. Start with any self-resentments you might have. Then move on to resentments related to externals. Take some time to make your list and add to it over the course of a week. When you are finished, set aside some time to start the process of letting go of these resentments. Find someone you feel comfortable with to voice your resentments and speak them aloud. If you don't feel comfortable voicing the resentment, read aloud to yourself. When you are finished, burn or destroy the list.

Tool: Let Them Pass

Creating space for people is an important way to practice compassion and consideration. Take some time throughout the day to practice humility. In doing so we stop making the world about us and begin to cooperate with the world we live in. We let go of the need to be right or first.

Here are a few examples:
1. Let someone cut in while you're in traffic, even if you're in a rush.
2. Open the door for someone, male or female.
3. Go out of your way to support a co-worker.
4. Allow for someone else's viewpoint without argument.
5. Try not to criticize, condemn, or complain.
6. Practice active listening.

MAXIM 4 – AMENDS AND GRATITUDE

amend
1. to modify, rephrase, or add to or subtract from
2. to change for the better; improve.
3. to remove or correct faults in; rectify.
4. to grow or become better by reforming oneself.[32]

We are a Work In Progress

We are not perfect! Although we work on improving our response, sometimes we still react emotionally. We are progressively better, but still guilty of mistakes. Every day we improve ourselves, the bar of acceptable behavior raises another level. The people closest to us are usually the most affected by the positive changes, as well as the negative outbursts. We have to stop and give ourselves credit for our growth, but at the same time remember to own our behavior and apologize sincerely. Asking for forgiveness is different than saying sorry! **Please forgive me, friends. I am a work in progress seeking improvement and I accept I'm not perfect!**
-TAC-

Much like resentments, amends start with ourselves. As we become more self-aware and conscious in our daily lives, we find it increasingly important to look inward first. This is a fundamental marker of growth and development. If we are aligned with our values and beliefs – we want to live a life of

---

[32] http://www.thefreedictionary.com/amend

authenticity – we need to start with ourselves before we look outward.

It is essential to forgive ourselves as well as others. If we are consistently self-critical and judgmental of our behavior, we will find it very difficult to keep from projecting these feelings onto others. We severely limit our capacity for forgiveness if we cannot forgive ourselves. Everyone makes mistakes. Everyone has done something that has hurt another person at some point. Most of us have hurt others many times. If we can find a place of compassion within ourselves, we can share this acceptance with everyone in our lives.

Wild Geese
You do not have to be good.
You do not have to walk on your knees
for a hundred miles through the desert, repenting.
You only have to let the soft animal of your body
love what it loves.
Tell me about your despair, yours, and I will tell you mine.
Meanwhile the world goes on.
Meanwhile the sun and the clear pebbles of the rain
are moving across the landscapes,
over the prairies and the deep trees,
the mountains and the rivers.
Meanwhile the wild geese, high in the clean blue air,
are heading home again.
Whoever you are, no matter how lonely,
the world offers itself to your imagination,
calls to you like the wild geese, harsh and exciting --
over and over announcing your place
in the family of things.
-Mary Oliver-

Making Amends

Reach out and make amends if you feel the need. No need to be specific, just authentic and sincere. Do not be attached to the way it is received. This is not the point. You are making amends with yourself and the external. Simply do so from a place of compassion and let it go. When we make amends it must come from our powerful self. Our powerless self may need the forgiveness of others or may be holding on to self-pity by feeling sorry for their behaviors or our own.

"How you feel about the past--contentment or pride, versus bitterness or shame--depends entirely on your memories."[33]

We know from Maxim 2, *Self-Audit*, that we always have a choice. This is especially true when it comes to processing resentment through making amends and practicing gratitude. We decide how we feel about our past. We have a choice to practice forgiveness and to make amends. Reparation is the right thing for us to do, and for no other reason. We do it because we are powerful.

A powerful tool for forgiveness is the REACH concept developed by Dr. Everett Worthington. Dr. Worthington developed this tool as a result of his own personal experience with the brutal death of his mother. This is not a theoretical, academic tool. This comes from his head and his heart.

R – recall
E – empathize
A – altruistic
C – commit
H – hold

---

[33] "Authentic Happiness" Seligman p.75

To *recall* is to remember the hurt as realistically as possible, without any judgment. *Empathize* with the person who caused you harm, and try to understand the pain or suffering they may have had to do such a thing. *Altruistic* amends are based on forgiveness, without expectation. *To commit* is to make this amend publicly, either to the person or to someone you know. *Hold* is to hold on to the forgiveness; you don't need to forget the event, but you remember your forgiveness of the event.[34]

Shame

> "*In a culture of shame, we are constantly overwhelmed with feelings of fear, blame and disconnection. This creates an 'us and them' world. There are people like us, and then there are 'those other people.'*"[35]

If we want to dissolve shame in our lives, we do so by connecting to it. When we connect to our own shame and the shame we share with others, we eliminate the conditions for shame to flourish. We respond with understanding, empathy and compassion. We avoid being sympathetic, critical or taking pity on ourselves and others. We stay with the feeling and take a good look at what is underneath it. We relate to it and therefore it loses its potency.

Any time we start to separate ourselves from others through judgment, we are disconnecting ourselves from the world and from ourselves. The things we don't like about others are often the parts of us we don't like or are ashamed of. Let's give ourselves and everyone around us a break. By softening our response to the world, we let ourselves off the hook just as much. When we shame others, we perpetuate a cycle of shame. Shaming behavior is isolating. It makes us feel as if we don't belong or we don't fit in.

---

[34] "Authentic Happiness" Seligman, pp.79-81
[35] "I Thought It was Just me (But It Isn't)" Brown, p.145

Everyone deserves the opportunity to be themselves, to try and to fail as many times as it takes to learn and grow into the best version of themselves. Shame creates fear of failure, fear of others, and renders us powerless in the process. If we begin to stop participating in self-shaming and shaming others, we provide space for growth and development.

I want freedom for the full expression of my personality.
-Gandhi-

Acceptance

Accepting who you are, right now in this moment, isn't always easy. Depending on your mood, you might feel exceedingly good about who you are, or pretty disappointed, or anything in between. We want to get beyond what our emotional state is telling us and get to our core values and beliefs. To take the most honest approach we can and accept whatever we find.

We all know we cannot change the past. What we can do is determine what we need to shift or change in order to create the possibility for a more desirable future. Without acceptance, we may be forever influenced by our personal history. We can decide to shift and change who we are at any time. It's as easy as remembering Heraclitus' river. Change happens all the time, with or without us.

Many times when we make changes and accomplish things in our life, we do not have to wait for a certification period. The shift and change takes place immediately from the point of thought. The length of time in which we hold the thought increases the focus period, and as long as we repeat with aligned physical-mental-spiritual action, we are who we think we are.

The moment we make a change in our life, we are the person we present in that moment. The past doesn't correct itself, but it doesn't have to manifest in your current self. Take sobriety, for example:

> *every moment you are clean or sober, you are sober. The universe doesn't suggest any length of time for you to give yourself credit. Repeating the same focus and commitment over and over again improves your clarity, awareness and connection. We have not been restricted to a certain number of occurrences, any length of time, or requirements to qualify. Give yourself credit for who you are now, not what past experiences have shown you. The future will take care of itself and mirror your current state of consciousness!*
> **Change just happened.**
> **-TAC-**

Acceptance is a two-way street. When we practice acceptance, we accept ourselves and the people in our lives. If we make amends from a place of power, we do so without ego or expectation; rather, we do so because it feels right and it aligns with our values and beliefs. Making amends is a way of letting go of our past, letting go of the parts of our story that no longer serve or align with us.

Acceptance is our vehicle for peace and understanding. We find ourselves willing to give up the illusion of control. We can accept the fact that no matter how much energy we put into something, we do not ultimately control the result. What a relief from the internal pressure we place on ourselves! As a result, we start letting pressure off the world as well.

Self-Compassion

Self-compassion is just as crucial to making amends as it is in processing and understanding resentment. We need to be gentle with ourselves and make amends with our part. It is nearly impossible to practice forgiveness without compassion. If we cannot cultivate self-compassion, we will be hard-pressed to forgive ourselves for our past behaviors. Without compassion, we are unable to relate to ourselves and cannot stop the cycle of self-punishment for our past behaviors. Compassion allows us to make friends with our powerless self and understand we can learn and grow from our mistakes without being punished indefinitely.

Reminding ourselves over and over again how poor our past behaviors were does not allow us to move on and prevent them in the future. If we can let go of our expectation that we need to be perfect all the time, or that we need to do everything right the first time, we give ourselves space to grow and learn. Failure allows us to learn. Failure is an essential part of risk. It is also a tremendous gift as it allows us to see what we need to work on. It exposes us to new ways of thinking about and doing things in our lives. Failure is fundamental to the evolution of humanity. Failure is the birthplace of innovation.

> *"I have not failed. I've just found 10,000 ways that won't work."*
> **-Thomas A. Edison-**

Compassion for Others

When we make amends, we are practicing compassion. We are giving the gift of forgiveness. We are letting ourselves and the people in our lives know they are loved and accepted. Our powerless self might feel "robbed" or taken advantage of if we forgive someone and do not get a thanks or amends in return.

This half-forgiveness does not come from a place of compassion; it comes from self-centeredness, because it is conditional. There is a note attached which says, "You owe me." It is a conditional gesture which requires the other person to accept blame and to feel judged or even shamed. This is not forgiveness; it is a form of subtle retribution.

The power in making amends is in its selflessness. It is forgiveness given for only one reason: because you want to. Because in your own heart you have forgiven yourself and you want to share it with others. You make amends because you feel connected and aligned, internally and externally. You make amends through creating a clear and connected relationship to the situation, without judgment, blaming or otherwise holding any conditional requirements over the situation. It is an act of kindness, compassion and love in its purest form.

Empathy

> *"Empathy is the experience of understanding another person's condition from their perspective. You place yourself in their shoes and feel what they are feeling."*[36]

When we can let go of resentment and make amends, we do so because we have found a way to empathize. Our ability to connect to the world has grown to a higher level. We no longer see ourselves as better or worse than others. We are beginning to understand we are valuable just as we are, neither more nor less valuable than anyone else, no more or less deserving of love and kindness.

We have found a way to understand how someone else might have felt in the event or situation. We realize we have probably felt the same way at some point in our lives. That we, too, have hurt people or made poor decisions many times in the past.

The solution is to connect to the situation. Unfortunately, our habitual response is often to withdraw, escape or distract. This is what leads to a triple reaction: resentment erodes our ability to forgive, which triggers shaming behavior. Empathy allows us to open up to the world, to understand we live a shared human experience. It is like we are beginning to take off our armor and put down our swords.

---

[36] http://www.psychologytoday.com/basics/empathy

Real fearlessness is the product of tenderness. It comes from letting the world tickle your heart, your raw and beautiful heart. You are willing to open up, without resistance or shyness, and face the world. You are willing to share your heart with others.[37]
-Chögyam Trungpa-

Gratitude

gratitude
1. the quality of being thankful; readiness to show appreciation for and to return kindness.[38]

How often we wish we were somewhere else. Fast-forwarding to the future or dwelling in the past. We overlook the fortune in front of us. The fortune of this very moment is discarded in favor of what we hope will happen or wish could happen. Well, it's happening in this very moment.
I am in the Right place, at the Right time, Right now.
-TAC-

To practice gratitude, we start with being grateful for our precious human life. No one knows exactly what happens after we die. What we can be certain of is that we have this life to live. What we choose to do with this life is our decision. If we believe life sucks or life is unfair, we are telling ourselves we resent our life. When we are grateful for the life we are given, we see life as a gift.

Life is not a problem; it is a challenge and, ultimately, an amazing opportunity. When we are born we have infinite

---

[37] "Shambhala: The Sacred Path of The Warrior" Trungpa, p. 46
[38] https://www.google.com/search?q=gratitude+definition&oq=gratitude+d efini&aqs=chrome.1.69i57j0l5.9499j0j4&sourceid=chrome&espv=210&es_sm= 93&ie=UTF-8

possibilities as to how our life will unfold. If we value life, one of our fundamental healthy beliefs is that we affirm life is precious. In Buddhism there is an interesting concept about how unique it is to be born a human:

> *The human rebirth is said to be extremely rare. The Majjhima Nikaya (129 Balapandita Sutta) compares it to a wooden cattle-yoke floating on the waves of the sea, tossed this way and that by the winds and currents. The likelihood of a blind turtle, rising from the depths of the ocean to the surface once in a hundred years, putting its head through the hole in the yoke is considered greater than that of a being in the animal realm, hungry ghost realm or hell realm achieving rebirth as a human.[39]*

A famous TED Talk by Mel Robbins goes on to say the odds of you being born in the time you were born as the person you are today is 1 in 400 trillion. Of course there are many different ways to statistically analyze the situation, but Dr. Ali Binazir goes even farther. He calculates the odds of your parents meeting, the odds of them getting pregnant, the odds of a specific sperm fertilizing a specific egg, and the probability of your ancestors reproducing at 1 in 10 to the 2,685,000[th].[40]

No matter how you choose to look at it, we are miraculous. As far as we know, we are the only planet in the universe with any life on it. The fact that life evolved into a conscious being such as a human is indeed incredible. A different meteor strike or any rather normal cosmological event could have altered the course in any number of directions.

If we start our gratitude practice by being grateful for the life we are given, being grateful for every aspect of our

---

[39]http://en.wikipedia.org/wiki/Human_beings_in_Buddhism
[40]http://www.huffingtonpost.com/dr-ali-binazir/probability-being-born_b_877853.html

life is a natural progression. We can see how we can even be grateful for the difficulties we have faced and for the traumas we have endured. We realize everything is part of this incredible human existence and we are grateful for it. We can be grateful for the resentments we have held and the amends we have made. We are grateful for the lessons in all of it.

Problem→Challenge→Opportunity

Gratitude is not reserved for only the things we view as favorable or pleasant. When practiced properly, it is a mindset encompassing every aspect of our lives, including the failures. In many ways we are most grateful for the "problems" we face in our lives. Although they may be unpleasant, painful or scary, they teach us valuable lessons. These problems are not to be avoided. If we are grateful for everything in our lives, we see these problems as challenges.

When we are challenged, we face an opportunity for growth – an opportunity to discover areas we might need to work on in our character. We find the need to develop new skills to face these challenges. Sometimes we may simply confirm how powerful we are by facing these challenges and turning them into opportunities.

Some might say these are simply different words and do not change the reality of difficult situations in our lives. The reality is, these words shift our perspective. We have learned how powerful words are, especially the words we speak to ourselves and others. By identifying anything as a problem, it becomes something to be avoided. Simply seeing something as a challenge improves our relationship to it, but we may still want to avoid the situation if we are not feeling up to the challenge. Opportunities, however, are seen as positive and desirable; therefore, we tend to embrace them with enthusiasm.

So let's consider these words more deeply:

prob·lem
1. a matter or situation regarded as unwelcome or harmful and needing to be dealt with and overcome.[41]

challenge
1. A call to take part in a contest or competition, especially a duel.
2. A task or situation that tests someone's abilities.[42]

opportunity
1. an appropriate or favorable time or occasion.
2. a situation or condition favorable for attainment of a goal.
3. a good position, chance, or prospect, as for advancement or success.[43]

As we progress from problem to challenge to opportunity, we can see the difference in our relationship to the situation. A problem is negative, unwelcome, harmful – something we have to deal with and get over. A challenge is a test; a situation where we find ourselves in a contest. Unfortunately, to succeed in facing a challenge for its own sake is to commit yourself to the next challenge. An opportunity, however, is a positive experience. It is favorable: "a chance...for advancement or success." Which of the three would you rather be a part of?

When we see the uncomfortable parts of our lives as things to be avoided or as bad luck, we build resentment

---

[41]https://www.google.com/search?q=problem&oq=problem&aqs=chrome.. 69i57j69i65l3j0l2.1720j0j4&sourceid=chrome&es_sm=122&ie=UTF-8   -q=problem+definition

[42]http://www.oxforddictionaries.com/us/definition/american_english/challenge

[43]http://dictionary.reference.com/browse/opportunity

toward these things. If we practice gratitude, we see these things as opportunities for growth and development.

> *Problems along the way are all part of the journey. We are strong individuals with colorful stories. When it doesn't seem to be going our way, the truth is that we are getting what we gave. We asked for this, or we need it. As crazy as it may seem at the time, the reality is, someday we will be able to reflect on it and embrace it, or maybe even laugh at the experience. No need to doubt the inevitable. We are unique because of our collective experiences. This life, this existence, is awesome! Some days may seem difficult, but just think about how amazing your character-building is going!*
> **Adversity is the journey building character.**
> **-TAC-**

Change Your Story Part I

This is how we begin the process of changing our story. In Maxim 2, *Self-Audit* we started to figure out the story we tell ourselves and other people about who we are. Once we are able to find out what that story is, we can begin to change it. Until we let go of our resentments toward ourselves and others, we are going to continue to tell ourselves a powerless and self-defeating story. As we start to let go of resentments, make amends, and practice gratitude, we change the story to a powerful narrative.

Our new story is no longer about what the world is doing to us, but is based on the opportunity life presents us in every moment. When we first start thinking about resentments, we struggle to see them as an opportunity to grow. When our powerful self emerges, we can see these things as part of our journey. We accept these resentments and are grateful for the things they taught us and teach us still. We see letting go of resentments and making amends as an opportunity. Letting go allows us to become more compassionate and to learn how to give the gift of forgiveness. Now our story is no longer self-limiting and powerless. Our story becomes support for the growth of our powerful self.

Do you see the way that tree bends?
Does it inspire?
Leaning out to catch the sun's rays
A lesson to be applied
Are you getting something out of this all encompassing trip?
You can spend your time alone, re-digesting past regrets, oh
Or you can come to terms and realize
You're the only one who can't forgive yourself, oh
Makes much more sense to live in the present tense
Have you ideas on how this life ends?
Checked your hands and studied the lines
Have you the belief that the road ahead ascends off into the light?
Seems that needlessly it's getting harder
to find an approach and a way to live
Are we getting something out of this all-encompassing trip?
You can spend your time alone re-digesting past regrets, oh
or you can come to terms and realize
you're the only one who cannot forgive yourself, oh
makes much more sense to live in the present tense.
"Present Tense" Eddie Vedder & Mike McCready

Exercise: Ten Acts of Forgiveness – Ten Acts of Gratitude

List ten things you want to make amends with. Consider how you would take action on these ten items to practice forgiveness. Start with yourself.

List ten things you are grateful for. Consider how you would like to take action on these ten items to practice gratitude. Start with yourself.

Use paper, a Word document, a social network post, a napkin, your hand, or graffiti on a bridge. Whatever you use, allow your mind to explore all of the greatness presented to you at this moment in time and space.

Let it flow: simple, complicated, honest, sincere, deep.

Tool: Observe What You Bring in

Whether you think you can, or you think you can't--you're right.
-Henry Ford-

Make note of the results of your actions. If we want to change the circumstances of our lives, we are the first part of any change. Self-awareness allows us to take an objective perspective on how we live our lives and the effect it has on the external world. For example, if we go about our day increasing the chaos around us, we can expect more chaos. If we live our lives in service, we will experience more gratitude both internally and externally. This is not a direct tit-for-tat concept where we expect everything to work out evenly all the time, but when we change our momentum, we will see our overall picture shift in that direction.

1. Do you notice a difference when you bring a negative or positive attitude to a situation?

2. How are your relationships affected when you only do things for the sake of personal gain?

3. How do people treat you if you are consistently aggressive and critical?

4. How do people respond to you when you are passionate?

5. What are the results when you are patient and kind?

6. How do conversations change when you listen more?

MAXIM 5 – SUSTAINABILITY

sustainability
*1. The ability to be sustained, supported, upheld, or
confirmed.*[44]

---

*When we least expect it, old habits can show up! As we create a
higher standard for ourselves and discover more growth, our baseline
changes. The baseline is the place we feel acceptable behavior can be
monitored from. What was once acceptable behavior may now fall
below our improved set of values. As we evolve and build our
character, we will experience setbacks, but the really cool thing is
that most of the time it's never as far back as it used to be. As we
raise our bar, we raise our expectations.*
It's about progress, not perfection!
-TAC-

In the first G8way Maxim we discovered our powerful
self. In Maxim 2, *Self-Audit* we learned about when our
powerful self is showing up and when our powerless self is
running the show. We became more aware of how and when
we slide into feeling powerless. In going beyond resentment
we remove one of our core barriers to engaging ourselves
with compassion and understanding in the world. Through
amends and gratitude, we are learning to practice
forgiveness. Sustainability, the focus of this chapter, is about
getting our powerful self to show up as often as possible to
help us maintain our authenticity.

---

[44] http://dictionary.reference.com/browse/sustainability

Why We Backslide

> *The mind prefers the suffering it knows over the joy it has not yet met.*
> *-TAC-*

At times, in spite of our best efforts or how hard we have worked to become more self-aware and to heal, we can get caught up. Our old habitual patterns can surface through stress or other triggers. Even seemingly simple things like a song or a smell or a situation can trigger old memories, feelings or behaviors. When this happens, it is as if we are hijacked. Our normal, steady, conscious state is overwhelmed with emotion and irrational thinking. There are many reasons this can occur.

The primary scientific explanation has to do with our higher and lower brain and the way they interact. Our cerebral cortex is the higher or more evolved part of our brain and is thought to be responsible for our rational/conscious thought processes. This is a part of the brain that is unique in its development in humans as opposed to other primates. The lower part of our brain contains the amygdala. This is one of the oldest and most primitive parts of our brain. It is responsible for more of our subconscious thoughts and emotions, while also having heavy involvement in our emotional state. It is connected to many of our negative or traumatic experiences.

The tough part is that our amygdala responds much faster than our cerebral cortex. We are emotionally "hooked" microseconds before our conscious/rational mind kicks in. Suddenly our neurochemistry is beginning to change and we are in the beginning of an emotional response. This is why we often think, "I'm not even sure how it happened. I really had no intention of doing 'x' and then suddenly I found myself doing it." This is why people who want to prevent poor behavior are told to have a plan or to avoid triggering environments in the first place. You may go into a situation with all of the best intentions and a great attitude, but quickly find yourself battling the desire to act out.

The way in which we can prevent getting "re-hooked" in the first place comes from sustained practice and increasing our self-awareness. Meditation has been found to help reduce the emotional gap between our emotional and rational minds. It also helps us to learn not to react quite so quickly to any stimulus in our lives. Learning to create space for ourselves and others is an important part of reducing the effect of this automatic emotional triggering we experience. Healthy processing of past traumas and emotional events will also reduce our triggering reflex. These instances do hold important cues to help us recognize where we might still need growth and development.

The discomfort we feel when we are emotionally triggered but consciously aware that we do not want to act on these emotions can feel like an internal boxing match. This discomfort is part of the process of growth. Every time we make a different choice when we are triggered, we create a new pathway in our brain. We are developing new behavioral patterns to replace the poor or unwanted behaviors of the past.

The improvement might be uncomfortable, especially at first, but it represents progress. As with so many kinds of healing it gets worse before it gets better. At least, at last, it is the difference between sustained chronic pain and the pain of change. Being overwhelmed by triggers and resentment is similar to chronic physical pain versus the soreness we feel after a good workout, the pain associated with building muscle strength.

Sensory Inputs

Who we are is heavily influenced by our environment, including people, places, and things. Whether our surroundings have a negative or a positive impact on us is in our control. The environment presents the opportunity to determine what aligns with our authenticity and organic self. Change your environment and change the results.
Go with the flow but choose the right one.
-TAC-

Many things are beyond our control, but what we choose to put into our body is something we can control. Our five senses are the gateway to our inner self. In a world where we experience constant stimuli, we may not be able to control everything we are exposed to, but we typically have many choices throughout the day. We certainly have a choice as to what we choose to focus our attention on and what we can choose to ignore.

In our home life, we can mostly control what inputs we are exposed to. The core differentiation is to avoid things that initiate a quick-fix dopamine (the reward hormone) response versus gratifying experiences that release neurotransmitters like oxytocin (the cuddle hormone). Things like video games provide intermittent random surges of dopamine because the rewards are unpredictable. This is similar to how people become addicted to gambling. If we seek too many activities which produce these dopamine responses, we eventually reach an addictive state.

By pursuing gratifying experiences such as conversing with someone we love, playing with children or enjoying a hobby, we build up oxytocin. This is the anti-dopamine as it does not lead to compulsive behavioral patterns and actually reduces the likelihood that one will become addicted to anything. We can take the time to use our sense of smell to our advantage, with flowers or scented candles or by preparing healthful foods. We can put on soothing or inspirational music. We can taste and eat whole natural fruits and vegetables. Over time, all of these things contribute to our wellbeing by reducing our triggering response and supporting our health.

Triggers

What comes into our body through the five senses has a profound impact on our inner state. There is a physical, mental and spiritual impact resulting from anything we encounter in our daily lives. Some of these inputs we can control and some we cannot. Cultivating our inner strength and wellbeing helps us to engage the inputs we don't control in a connected and healthy manner.

The more conscious we are in our daily lives, the more sensitive we become to the inputs we experience. At first we can feel almost raw and vulnerable as we begin to become more present. We begin to see things we never knew affected us and normally ignored. This is why sustaining a healthy state is important to our ability to manage our lives and maintain our authenticity, no matter the external circumstances.

Part of sustaining a healthy state is finding which events and stimuli enhance our wellbeing and determining those that do not align with us. Making good choices about what we put into our bodies can have a tremendous impact on how we feel and our overall health. The key to managing any situation is typically prevention. By maintaining a healthy and positive mind and body state, we become more resilient to stress and its effects, sometimes even turning stress into a tool we can use to improve our situation by feeding off the stress-induced hormonal responses to enhance our performance.

Stress is a crucial component of triggering poor behavior and cravings. Managing stress/initiating positive beliefs about stress is fundamental to wellbeing, preventing poor behavioral responses. Stress can act as the magnifying glass for your internal state at any given time. It can catalyze both positive and negative internal feelings and emotions.

Specific stress-inducing triggers occur every day at the office, at mealtimes, and during the commute. They cannot be avoided, but our reaction to them can change by realizing how they affect us and taking the appropriate actions in our lifestyle to manage acute and chronic stress.

Getting Stuck...

It's possible I am pushing through solid rock
in flintlike layers, as the ore lies, alone;
I am such a long way in I see no way through,
and no space: everything is close to my face,
and everything close to my face is stone.
I don't have much knowledge yet in grief
so this massive darkness makes me small.
You be the master: make yourself fierce, break in:
then your great transforming will happen to me,
and my great grief cry will happen to you.
-Rainer Maria Rilke, "Pushing Through" transl. Robert Bly

Everything has been going great. We are feeling so good about our growth and development. We are experiencing profound insights into our relationship to the world and...then....nothing.....seems......to.......be.........happeni ng. We feel as if we are stuck, simply running in place. We are putting in the effort to live an intentional life day in and day out, yet we feel as if we are going nowhere. We are feeling many of the same things we have felt before, with no sign of growth or improvement. In these times, if we can honestly say we are putting in our best effort and maintaining our authenticity, we are likely experiencing the integration of our previous growth.

Like performance plateaus faced by weightlifters or musicians, our mental and spiritual growth also reach equilibrium and level out as we adapt to the changes in our lives. Our minds take time to integrate any new developments or mental shifts, or to absorb any emotional processing we have gone through. This is when faith and patience are crucial. If the changes you have made in your life have benefitted you previously, don't lose faith now. If the gains are not as profound or accelerated as they were in the past, it doesn't mean they are any less effective or necessary. These periods of feeling stuck are typically when the growth is taking root and starting to cross over the mind/body resistance to change, finally dissolving old beliefs and behavioral patterns.

Mindfulness

Practicing mindfulness is fundamental to learning how to stay present. When things are difficult or uncomfortable, we usually look for a way out. In Maxim 2, *Self-Audit* we discussed many ways in which we try to escape from our emotional state. One of the best ways we can train to process emotions and maintain a healthy mental state is to practice mindfulness.

Meditation is the primary method we can use in order to help train our mind. It doesn't have to be a formal meditation practice; it can be as simple as sitting still, quietly focusing on our breath. Quiet contemplation is a form of mindfulness. The key is to reduce our sensory inputs and external influences to allow ourselves time to sit still and connect to our internal state.

Science has begun to prove that meditation has tangible effects on our emotional health and wellbeing. In their research on mindfulness-based cognitive therapy (MCBT), Mark Williams and Danny Penman uncovered numerous benefits to mindfulness practice.

87

- Anxiety, depression and irritability all decrease with regular sessions of meditation. Memory also improves, reaction times become faster and mental and physical stamina increase
- People who meditate enjoy better and more fulfilling relationships
- Studies worldwide have found that meditation reduces the key indicators of chronic stress, including hypertension
- Meditation has also been found to be effective in reducing the impact of serious conditions, such as chronic pain and cancer, and can even help to relieve drug and alcohol dependence
- Studies have recently shown that meditation bolsters the immune system and thus helps to fight off colds, flu, and other diseases.[45]

As far as the benefits are concerned, there may not be a single better practice we can use to enrich our health than mindfulness. It helps us to better integrate our emotions and improves our overall health substantially. It doesn't cost anything and there are benefits from doing it for even five minutes per day. We consider it to be an essential part of any effective lifestyle-support regimen.

Below we discuss the second part of our daily actions as an important component of sustaining our powerful self. We discussed the physical actions in Maxim 1, *Powerful Celebration*. For sustainability, we add our mental actions to help us maintain our psychological wellbeing.

---

[45] "Mindfulness – An Eight Week Plan For Finding Peace in a Frantic World" Williams, Penman, p.6

Daily Actions – Mental - Read, Meditate, Journal

1. *Read* – This aligns with eating as a way to nourish the mind on a daily basis. Human beings thrive on knowledge and learning. Reading helps to enrich our personal experience and bring new thoughts and ideas into our consciousness. Fiction, non-fiction, magazines, and journals all help to provide us with daily nourishment for our minds. Of course, much like food, what we choose to read will determine its effect on our health.

2. *Meditate* – We need sleep to help our bodies to rest and repair. While we are awake, meditation provides the same support. A daily meditation practice brings us into the present moment and increases our awareness. Meditation has proven to be one of the most potent stress management tools available to us. The great thing is, we can do it anytime, anywhere. Take some time to sit still, breathe and listen. It's that simple.

3. *Journal* – This is our mental exercise. Keeping a journal helps us to process the experiences of our lives. Writing helps to engage the mind in a connected state, enabling us to bring mindfulness to our daily lives. A journal can help us sort out difficult emotional experiences or aid us in making good decisions. Reflection is an essential aspect of mental and spiritual health. Just start writing! There are no rules.

Lifestyle

Through our daily actions we are building the framework for a lifestyle which sustains our health and wellbeing. We have created our version based on what we have found to be helpful and based on the feedback of others we have worked with over the years. What is important is for everyone to find a daily routine that works for them. Nearly all healthy and successful people have created a system like this to sustain their health and wellbeing.

If we choose to engage in an ongoing process of growth, it requires sustainable physical, mental and spiritual energy. Just as an athlete requires proper sleep, nutrition and exercise in order to perform at a high physical level, spiritual athletes require proper training, nourishment and rest. The difference is, we choose to integrate our lifestyle physically, mentally, and spiritually to maintain proper balance.

Will Is Not Enough

To help us find clarity and perspective, we can use various concepts and tools to help us determine our true values and reshape our beliefs accordingly. When we align our values and beliefs, actions follow. People often struggle trying to change their lives by focusing solely on their actions or behavior. They feel as if they simply need to change the things they do, or their outer environment, and everything will get better. This is mostly ineffective as people consistently find they are relying almost entirely on pure will to accomplish this behavioral change. There is internal resistance due to self-defeating or irrational beliefs they are clinging to.

Will is a finite resource for all of us. As we go about our day, we use our reserve of willpower along the way. As we make various decisions, big and small, we call upon our will. Willpower is a skill, something we can grow and expand, but if we have conflicting values and beliefs, willpower will never be enough. Our willpower will become exhausted by this internal struggle.

By aligning our values and beliefs, we require less will power to make good decisions – authentic decisions – which align with our powerful self. We can now begin to use our willpower for growth and expansion. We can use it to stretch our comfort zone, rather than to merely keep us afloat in the sea of our status quo. We can eventually become more "skilled" in terms of self-control/willpower.

As you become skilled in a task, its demand for energy diminishes. Studies of the brain have shown that the pattern of activity associated with an action changes as skill increases, with fewer brain regions involved.[46]

To some degree it can be said we are inherently lazy. We will take the path of least resistance. This can be a form of great efficiency in some situations. However, when the conflict is between our values and beliefs, the easy way usually leads to choosing poor coping mechanisms to help us deal with this inner conflict. The easy way is to simply not deal with the conflict and look for escape or distraction.

Sustaining Motivation – Positive Attitude

There is no other road to genius than through voluntary self effort![47]
-Napoleon Hill-

Our motivation to sustain our evolution comes from within. It is sustained by our passion to bring the best version of ourselves to the world. Bringing our A-game, we try to realize our purpose and enjoy the freedom to be our true authentic self in every moment.

Our primary motivation is derived from our core values. Sustaining motivation can be difficult when we feel as if we are not making any progress. When we find ourselves really struggling to find the energy to live an intentional life, we

---

[46] "Thinking Fast and Slow" Kahneman, p.35
[47] "Think And Grow Rich" Hill, p.152

must rely on faith and patience. Our powerless self often shows up when we find ourselves wondering if it's all really worth it. We start asking internal questions like, "Why not just escape or take a break from life?" There's a difference between knowing we need some time to recharge, versus wanting to escape, and we all know the difference between the two.

Our motivation wanes when we start to feel as if we "should" be making more progress or reaping greater rewards. This is the trap of reward-based thinking. When we engage in this type of thinking, we do not act according to our values and beliefs; instead, we act based on expected outcomes. This is another form of externalizing, whereby we are externalizing the reward for our effort. It is not enough to find satisfaction in living authentically; instead, we seek some form of external pleasure or validation. This shifts us back into the hamster wheel of thinking we can find true joy and happiness outside ourselves.

One of the most famous theories of motivation is Maslow's hierarchy of needs. They are broken down into categories from most basic, such as air, food and sleep, to higher spiritual needs like self-fulfillment and personal growth. The higher needs in Maslow's hierarchy are internally motivated and considered to be the most fulfilling. We would differ in our opinion of the need for self-esteem to be externalized, as he suggests; however, his hierarchy gives us some insight into human motivation. The most enduring motivation comes from within.

When we have faith in ourselves and the patience to be present and connected to our lives, we can sustain our motivation by simply knowing our authenticity will provide us with the right direction in life. We act because we want to engage the world and grow, not because we expect a specific reward or acknowledgement from externals. We can be content to receive gifts or acknowledgement, but we are not dependent on these rewards to motivate us.

> *The rewards of living life clean of addiction, destructive behavior, and emotional turmoil are physical, mental, and spiritual health. The benefit is that the people, places, and things around you fall in place for you and opportunities, love, and abundance find you. The result is that you feel happiness and fulfillment. It all starts with us!* **It's all here right now. All we have to do is take care of ourselves!**
> **-TAC-**

patience

1. the bearing of provocation, annoyance, misfortune, or pain without complaint, loss of temper, or anger.

2. an ability or willingness to suppress restlessness or annoyance when confronted with delay.

3. quiet, steady perseverance; even-tempered care; diligence.[48]

Patience is a character trait we cultivate over time. For most of us it does not come naturally. From childhood, our first instinct is to take the course of action which will produce immediate results. It is in the delaying of gratification, however, that we practice and cultivate patience.

This is another example of using our conscious mind to override the urges of our emotional mind. We are drawn initially to instant gratification, yet we often benefit far more from delaying gratification. Intentional living is a long exercise of patience in many respects. It takes a tremendous amount of patience to be accountable in every moment and live authentically.

---

[48] http://www.thefreedictionary.com/patience

perseverance

1. steadfastness in doing something despite difficulty or delay in achieving success.[49]

Perseverance is at the core of sustaining motivation. It is a character trait we can develop over time through practice. It is taking an extra step when we don't feel like it. It is being accountable even when it might cause us some pain and suffering. When we strive to live an intentional life in spite of the infinite number of distractions we face, we grow faith in ourselves. We become more and more capable by facing adversity and seeing trials as an opportunity to learn.

You may encounter many defeats, but you must not be defeated. In fact, it may be necessary to encounter the defeats, so you can know who you are, what you can rise from, how you can still come out of it.
-Maya Angelou-

When we pursue our passion, we will face obstacles. These are the moments when we gain the necessary experience to achieve our goals. If we see these things as reasons to quit, we increase the resistance internally. The obstacle becomes larger, more challenging and typically more uncomfortable. This can lead to acting out in unhealthy ways and is often at the root of most of our self-destructive behaviors. If we decide to take a different route when we face adversity, we can change our habitual response to it. Over time, not only do we see the opportunity that is available to us, but we can come to look forward to the challenge.

---

[49]https://www.google.com/search?q=perseveerence&oq=perseveerence&aqs=chrome..69i57j0l5.2154j0j7&sourceid=chrome&espv=210&es_sm=122&ie=UTF-8 - q=perseverance&spell=1

Challenging times bring stress and difficult emotions. Making poor decisions during these times creates a poor behavioral pattern. Using substances, spending too much money or indulging our emotions sets the stage for our brain to expect the same in future situations. If we choose to make good decisions during difficult times in our lives, we begin a new pattern, which will create a new expectation for our mind, body and spirit in the future. Next time things get tough, create a new habit and treat yourself kindly as the first step in managing the situation.
Bad times do not have to bring bad decisions.
-TAC-

Exercise: Eight Week Opportunity

In Maxim 2, *Self Audit,* we made a commitment to experience clarity for four weeks. Sustainability is about continuing our momentum over time. The eight week opportunity is an extension of our previous commitment.

What goals or projects would you like to complete in the next two months? Select well-defined and realistic-while-somewhat-challenging goals that reflect your core values. Think in terms of what attracts you rather than what you think you should do.

1. What personal characteristics am I concerned with?
2. What personal characteristics will I present to the world?
3. What activities or actions will I eliminate?
4. What activities or actions will I add to my life?

Now let us commit to our physical and mental daily actions for the next eight weeks.

Physical
- Sleep
- Eat
- Exercise

Mental
- Read
- Meditate
- Journal

Take some time to track each of the six daily actions over the next eight weeks. Give yourself one point for each daily action performed in a given day. An additional point is earned when you abstain from a behavior you chose to eliminate. Another point is earned when you engage in any positive behavior you chose to add.

You can earn up to eight points per day. Tally them up at the end of eight weeks to see how far you've come. Once you finish the eight weeks, try it again and see if you can beat your score!

56 days x 8 points per day = Maximum points 448

Tool: Self Check-In

The self check-in is a three-step process to help you realign yourself when you feel out of sorts or off-balance. If you feel like you're "spinning," this is a great tool to help you find your center.

1. *Recognition*
You might feel "in the pits," "struggling," "pink cloud," "over-excited," "stuck," etc.

Physical – Hungry, tired, injured, low energy, sick, hurt, ugly, frumpy;

Mental – angry, sad, depressed, scared, frustrated, overwhelmed, insecure, lonely, anxious, irrational;

Spiritual – disconnected, bored, disillusioned, purposeless, hopeless, judgmental, complaining, shaming, blaming, unsympathetic, resentful, lost;

Behaviors – compulsive, impulsive, pleasure-seeking, addicted, withdrawn, anti-social, food and TV bingeing, wanting to escape, oversleeping, unwashed, unkempt, late or absent from work, shirking responsibility, procrastinating, making bad sexual choices, avoiding loved ones

2. *Self-Audit*
Analyze the triggers: How are you being affected by externals in your recent experience?

Journal Exercise: *Drill Down* – Start with something you want to explore – an event, a feeling, a thought. Journal for ten minutes without censoring or correcting or rewriting. It doesn't have to make sense or be coherent. It's sloppy copy. Take some time to skim what you just wrote and look for the main theme/concept/idea. Journal again for ten more minutes without censorship and skim the content again. Do this three or four times total.

3. Re-Alignment
1. How do you get back to this moment? Be present.
2. Meditate.
3. Practice daily actions.
4. Give yourself a break. Let it go. Learn from the experience. Don't repeat.
5. Practice self-compassion.
6. Cultivating patience/practicing acceptance.
7. Gratitude – These moments/phases are an opportunity to catch a glimpse into what might still need work or reconciliation. Find the takeaway or lesson.

Maxim 6 – Dream Design and Visualization

dream
1. *a series of images, ideas, emotions, and sensations occurring involuntarily in the mind during certain stages of sleep.*
2. *a daydream; a reverie.*
3. *a state of abstraction; a trance.*
1. *to have a deep aspiration.*
2. *to regard something as feasible or practical*
3. *to conceive of; imagine.*[50]

Now that we have experienced some clarity, it is relatively easy to allow our minds the freedom and courage to dream about our future. Active dreaming as opposed to daydreaming is to envision our optimum outcome while awake. Picture being the individual you always wanted to be. Think about the interests that light you up with joy. Maybe you are living your dream, or maybe as life changes, your dream has an opportunity to change.

Dream about your future relationships, career, and service to the community. Where do you picture yourself? Many times in life we practice being responsible, hardworking and people-pleasing for so long that as adults, we lose our inherent gift of dreaming. Perhaps we can remember the freedom to dream beyond limitation we may have experienced as a child.

1. Was there something you wanted to be?
2. Did you always imagine yourself in a different place?
3. With a certain person?
4. Or in a specific career?

---

[50] http://www.thefreedictionary.com/dream

99

5. What did you see as a child, before you experienced failure, discipline, and skepticism?

Sometimes we wonder if we will ever do the things we really want to do. Is it even possible? Do I have what it takes? These questions give you a quick answer. They let you off the hook and they create a result. The result is procrastination and doubt. Dreaming will never hurt you. Creating a path forward for yourself will never hurt you. Believing in yourself will never hurt you. Receiving the results of your dreams will never hurt you. There will be challenges along the way. If you accept these challenges as opportunities, you will see they are part of the process. Sometimes the challenges provide you with more than the end result!
Dream, create, believe, receive!
-TAC-

Dream YOUR Dream

The universe is waiting for your next request. The universe works for you. It works for us all. Our key to success is right between our ears. We can unleash the power just by thinking. While some things take longer than others, little miracles are at hand. Start off small and experience minor miracles, then when you're convinced there's really something cool going on, try something bigger. Why not start off by asking for belief? When you begin to believe, you begin to turn the key. The possibilities are endless.
-Dave Blake Sr.-
-TAC-

In Maxim 2, *Self-Audit*, we discussed discovering our own internal truth. By aligning our values and beliefs, we can take a step towards living authentically. Dream design is to be engaged from this unique, authentic place. This is your opportunity to dream from your heart, to set your mind, body and soul free to pursue any thoughts or desires you choose. Stay focused on what you want to bring into your life. Align yourself with what works.

Don't focus on things you don't want, even behaviors or traits you want to eliminate. Let those things drop away as you engage in behavior that moves you toward your goals.

Objective: Open your mind to the possibilities. The most difficult part of dreaming is realizing it is OK to dream.

When we focus on "your" dream, what we mean is to leave the externals out of it. Many of our dreams, goals or desires are influenced by external factors, such as what might make other people happy or societal expectations of what is considered successful. It is not that we choose to take a cavalier attitude, unconcerned how our dreams affect the external world, but we do not make these things part of our dreaming process. Dreaming is unique and personal to us. When we move toward creating a plan of action, we begin the process of making our dreams tangible and can then take any necessary externals into consideration.

Fantasy vs. Dreaming

fantasy
(psychology)
a. a series of pleasing mental images, usually serving to fulfill a need not gratified in reality.
b. the activity of forming such images.[51]

It is important to make a distinction between dreaming and fantasy or daydreaming. In some ways they are very similar. Dreaming is certainly allowing ourselves to move beyond our perceived boundaries or realities, to let our

---

[51] http://www.thefreedictionary.com/fantasy

minds flow freely. For our purposes, the distinction is that fantasy is more of an attempt to use our mind to capture a feeling or desire we are unable to obtain in our lives. Fantasy is typically not rooted in our own authenticity, but comes from a place of desire or wishing. It is often derived from a version of ourselves we "wish we were" versus who we truly are at our core. Fantasy distorts and is distorted by the external world, and is not a part of our internal truth.

Fantasy can also describe the thoughts and feelings we generate when we worry and start to form hypothetical situations about our future. "If I don't get X, then Y will happen." The reality is, we cannot predict our lives so absolutely in any given moment. As humans we crave certainty. We have a natural tendency to try to predict the future, but we need to realize these predictions are nothing more than fantasy. Dreaming is about getting closer to our internal truth and beginning to create a picture of how to live that truth. We can say dreaming is more about getting closer to our inner needs and wants, while fantasy is often about outer wants and desires.

Fantasy tends to surround thoughts of pleasure and escape. It lacks any sense of the present moment. When done in a healthy and authentic manner, dreaming has a sense of presence to it: listening to what your internal voice is trying to tell you. Imagine what living your truth can be and, when you get to visualization, how it can feel. Dreaming is more aligned with producing a gratifying experience, versus pleasure only.

Pleasure vs. Gratification

We want to make a distinction here between pleasurable and gratifying experiences. Most of us blend these two things together as one and the same. We feel as if seeking pleasure is a reasonable and healthy basis for decision-making. We want to be happy and we equate pleasure with happiness. If we dig a little deeper, we will see pleasure is not what truly makes us happy and fulfilled; rather, it is the gratifying experience we find truly rewarding.

Pleasure is primarily a pleasant sensory and emotional sensation, a good feeling we get from certain activities. These feelings are often short-lived and require constant and increasing stimuli to maintain. This need to increase a diminishing pleasure occurs over time as we develop addictive and compulsive behaviors. Getting high or drunk initially feels good, but it lacks any expression of our authenticity. It doesn't engage us at a core level and therefore its effects are temporary and ultimately unfulfilling. To maintain the same level of pleasure, we must engage in the activity more frequently and with greater intensity over time. Pleasurable experiences often end in disappointment, with feelings of guilt and/or shame.

Gratifying experiences, on the other hand, are a result of expressing ourselves through our activities. When we feel gratified by our experiences, we feel a sense of connectedness and accomplishment as well as a good or pleasant feeling. The satisfaction we feel from a gratifying experience is enduring and almost never contains any feelings of shame or guilt. Gratifying experiences do not require increasing intensity and frequency over time in order to maintain the feeling of fulfillment we obtain from them.

This pleasure-gratification distinction mirrors the distinction between fantasy and dreaming. In a sense, we can see pleasure aligning itself with fantasy and gratification aligning itself with dreaming. Fantasy is an attempt to seek pleasure or instant relief from your current state. Dreaming is a way to connect to our authentic self through our mind with the goal of living a life of fulfillment and gratification.

No limits – No Boundaries

The garden of the world has no limits, except in your mind.[52]
-Rumi-

Our current situation may sometimes limit us and we may need to dig deeper to find the true reasons for the dream. Now is the time to dream without limitations. We all have a dream and sometimes it's planted deep within our minds. Unfortunately, the self-defeating mind can challenge us by not even allowing us to consider the possibilities. The distraction may come in several forms: "I'm too old," or, "That sounds crazy!" or, "It would be too difficult," we might say.

Dreaming has no guidelines or expectations. Dreaming is not to be confused with a plan of action. Dreaming is allowing your core values to play or flirt, take flight and experience what aligns with your inner truth. Let your organic self show up and experience your organic truth. We all have dreams and fears. Dreaming freely allows us to imagine and listen to our truth.

Too often we settle for less and don't think twice about it. We simply accept that we're just one of those people that aren't meant to be happy. We've been this way so long it has become our way of life. It's our *modus operandi*, our habit that seems to be our character. Well, here's a news flash: it doesn't have to be that way and we weren't put here to settle for less. Happiness is achievable if we just focus our minds toward it.

Unlike negative emotion, which narrows our repertoire to fight the immediate threat, positive emotion advertises growth.[53]

---

[52] http://www.goodreads.com/quotes/tag/limits
[53] "Authentic Happiness" Seligman, p. 209

The greatest challenges in life are often the limits we place on ourselves. We doubt our ability and potential to achieve our dreams by deciding in advance they are not possible, at least not right now. These limits are created by our own insecurity and personal history, bolstered by fear of failure or pain that lingers from the past. Yet we do not acknowledge the wisdom and character we have gained from these experiences. Instead of looking at the past as a way to limit yourself, think about all the great things you learned and how they will increase your chances of success today.

Instead of worrying about how things might not work if you take a chance, relish the opportunity to learn more about yourself and others if things *don't* work out the way you want. When we are dreaming, we are not trying to be realistic or practical. We are opening ourselves up to endless possibilities. Dreaming helps us to expand beyond our boundaries. It is a process to help us get closer to our own authenticity.

Resistance to Your Dreams

Sometimes it's difficult to believe that your dreams and vision will come to fruition. One reason is that we often look at past failures as examples of future outcome. If the dream aligns with your organic truth, then it's safe to believe all of the actions between now and the destination will present you with new results. Don't spend any time connecting your previous experiences with the journey. Buckle up, believe, and enjoy the road!
Previous outcomes represent nothing in the future.
-TAC-

Drop Your Story Part I

One of the great aspects of dreaming is our ability to drop our storyline while we are dreaming. Dreaming allows us to let go of or take a break from our limiting beliefs. If we are fully engaged in dreaming without any boundaries, we are not confined by our past. We don't need to discuss with ourselves whether or not we are ready or able to live the life we are dreaming about. Dreaming doesn't require any specific qualifications. Everyone has the right and the ability to dream. Drop any negative self-talk or limiting beliefs while you engage in the process of dreaming.

I deeply and profoundly accept myself; there are no limitations.
-TAC-

In Maxim 2, *Self-Audit* we began the process of uncovering our story, to see what it is we tell ourselves every day about who we are and what we are capable of. In Maxim 4, *Amends and Gratitude* we start to change our story. We realize we don't have to live our lives based on our past or what other people expect of us. Now we can begin letting go of our story. We can let our story write itself in each moment as we live our lives. We no longer need to define who we are or what our place is in the world. We belong because we know we are good enough, simply because we were born. We are just as qualified as everyone else to live our lives authentically.

Fear and Uncertainty

The most difficult part of dreaming is realizing it is OK. We don't need any special qualifications to allow ourselves to dream. This sounds obvious, but many of us struggle to dream without fear and uncertainty creeping into our dreams. Dreaming doesn't require a specific resume, formal training or education. Still, we immediately begin to question our dreams. "Is this really possible?" "Can I really do this?" "What happens if I fail?" Our rational mind poses such questions to try to determine whether the contents of our dreams are real or feasible.

The idea is often expressed as right- or left-brain thinking. Science doesn't validate any "side" of the brain as having more influence on creative versus logical thinking, but we do certainly have logical and creative aspects to our minds.[54] We have parts of our lower brain which contain our emotional and subconscious mind, and parts of our higher brain which control rational and logical thought processes. The brain is highly integrated throughout all of its component parts.

When we dream, we are attempting to engage our creative, intuitive mind. By allowing ourselves the emotional freedom to detach from planning or rationalizing, we can let our more creative side take control of the dreaming process. It is very important to engage dreaming from this mental space as much as we possibly can. The rational, logical mind will play its role as we begin to visualize our dreams and eventually create a plan of action.

Visualization

visualization
1. the act or an instance of visualizing.
2. a technique involving focusing on positive mental images in order to achieve a particular goal.[55]

---

[54] http://www.huffingtonpost.com/2013/08/19/right-brain-left-brain-debunked_n_3762322.html
[55] http://www.collinsdictionary.com/dictionary/english/visualization

Visualization invites the opportunity for the universe to deliver us the reality we seek. Our powerful internal voice is running the show. Dreams come from that powerful place within us that as children we were free to explore and believe we could. Visualization is our first step toward discovery of our new reality. When we engage in visualization, it helps our mind to actually experience the dreams we want to manifest in our lives. Our subconscious mind doesn't really differentiate whether or not the experience is actually happening. Therefore, we positively reinforce our desired result.

> *You visualize [pitches]. You see it in your head; you think it…I used to play every pitcher in my mind before I went to the ballpark. I started getting ready for every game the moment I woke up.[56]*
> *-Hank Aaron-*

Visualization helps prepare our mind and body for success. It is the equivalent of psychological priming, yet it is self-priming as opposed to being influenced by external forces. Priming activates previous associations in our memory and can create a biased response. If we have been primed with a color like yellow, for example, and then we are asked to name a fruit, we are likely to respond with "banana." If we are visualizing our dreams actively, we prime ourselves to create and respond to these conditions in the future.

Be Present

When we begin the process of visualizing our dream, it is important to be present. Visualize the dream as if it is happening right now in the moment. This is not a process of

---

[56] https://sportpsychquotes.wordpress.com/tag/imagery/page/3/

"I'm going to" or "When I get to." Visualization helps us to familiarize our mind and body with our dreams and aspirations. We want to feel as if we are experiencing these things in as realistic a manner as possible. We visualize the life we dream about as if it is happening right now.

Position your body as if you were doing exactly what you would do in the situation or experience you are visualizing. If you have a dream to be on stage, then stand up as if you were performing. Visualize the theater, what it looks like, what it feels like, smell the popcorn. Engage as many senses as possible. Visualize the crowd and the applause. There's no need for any negativity in our visualization, and no need for fear or doubt. If you start to feel those things, then begin to visualize yourself without any fear or doubt.

The core component of visualization is to have total faith in your process and your ability to manifest your dreams. By remaining faithful to your vision, you send reinforcing messages to your conscious and subconscious mind. In many ways your brain doesn't know the difference between your visualization and an actual event. This is why visualization is so powerful and effective. You are preparing yourself to truly live these situations or events in the future.

Finding Your Mission

Sometimes we are faced with very difficult choices. We can be presented with opportunities which, on the surface, seem incredible. These opportunities may be in the form of more money, greater status, or even love. Finding clarity to help us make choices in these situations is very challenging. It requires us to look deeply into ourselves to determine what it is we truly need to be happy. Does this opportunity serve your soul purpose? If we just look at the surface, we may only see what we want to see instead of what we need to see.
Look inside for the answer.
-TAC-

After we have spent some time dreaming and visualizing our life as it aligns with our powerful self, we can reflect on the core components. Take some time to think about the core values and themes that are consistent in your dreaming and visualizing. There are many ways in which we might live our life according to these core values. By reflecting on these things, we can begin to see the things which make up our personal mission or "soul purpose." If you already have a clear understanding of what that means to you, then dreaming and visualizing is a way for you to move closer to fulfilling your mission.

For those of us who do not have a clear sense of mission or purpose, we can find the key aspects of our true passion from the process. We may also find that what we originally might have thought of as our dream job or ideal life is not necessarily the only path to a truly gratifying and joyful life. Maybe we always dreamed about being on stage, as we discussed earlier. Take some time and think about what it is we truly are passionate about in regard to being on stage. Do we enjoy connecting with people? Do we enjoy the creativity? Do we enjoy making people happy?

When dreaming and visualizing, we allow ourselves the freedom to pursue what is in our heart and mind without boundaries, without preconceptions, without other people's opinions and without our story. By doing so, we are able to tap into our powerful, authentic self and see what surfaces. When we do this, we get closer to the things which truly align with our uniqueness and our unique gifts to the world. When we find our mission or soul purpose, we can begin to take the necessary steps to live our lives accordingly.

Soul Purpose

Signature Strengths + Passion = Mission/Soul Purpose
-TAC-

Our mission, or soul purpose, is a combination of our signature strengths and our passion. We identified our signature strengths in Maxim 2, *Self-Audit* and now we can use them to help us to define our mission. Through our dreaming and visualizing we have found the things we are passionate about. These things are an extension of our core values and beliefs. When we combine them, we can see a clear picture of our unique mission in this life.

The purpose of dream design and visualization is to build your life around your personal mission. To begin creating a vision of what your life would look like if it was built around your unique gifts. Living an authentic life is profoundly easier when our life's work is in alignment with our personal mission. For example, we may no longer use excess energy compromising our values and beliefs in order to make a living. We may be using incredible amounts of our limited willpower going to work every day in a job which we are not passionate about. As a result, we feel drained by our life. In contrast, if our life is centered in our soul purpose, we regain our energy and find more joy in our daily life.

Finding Your Flow

The result of living authentically and aligning our life with our soul purpose is that we experience states of flow more often. Flow is a state of full engagement in whatever we are doing at that moment. In sports, flow is often described as the zone – when an athlete feels as if everything slows down and they are experiencing effortless peak concentration. We experience flow most often when we are engaged in activities that align with our authenticity.

Usually the more difficult a mental task, the harder it is to concentrate on it. But when a person likes what he does and

*is motivated to do it, focusing the mind becomes effortless
even when the objective difficulties are great.*[57]

One of the easiest ways to experience more flow is to build your life around your signature strengths. This is not to say we only choose to do things which come easily to us. We may be engaging in things which suit our signature strengths and still find ourselves to be challenged at a high level. This combination is most likely to produce a flow state. It is this blend of feeling as if you are challenged yet knowing you have what it takes to ultimately be successful in your task which produces greater joy in our lives.

Flow comes from working in alignment with our mission/soul purpose. When we feel challenged, engaged and competent, combined with a sense of fulfillment, flow is a nearly automatic response. These are the moments when we feel as if there is no sense of time. We may be working at an extremely high level, exerting tremendous amounts of energy and being highly productive, yet we do not feel drained. In fact, we often feel energized and motivated to engage every part of our lives with a sense of renewed enthusiasm.

---

[57]"Finding Flow" Csikszentmihalyi, p.27

Exercise: 8 Powerful Questions

Please take the time to answer these questions. The purpose of these questions is to expand yourself and eliminate boundaries.

1. What are your strongest beliefs about yourself and the world right now?

2. What gifts do you have that you would like to make available to the world?

3. When in your life did you feel the most creative?

4. When in your life were you most committed to something/someone?

5. What are the greatest accomplishments of your life?

6. About what have you taken the strongest stand?

7. What is the most important lesson you have learned to date? What bit of wisdom would you share with the world?

8. What gets you excited? What are you passionate about?

Tool: Vision Board

Creating a visual representation of your personal vision and dreams helps to bring them to fruition. When you write them out, a part of you is making a commitment and taking the first actionable step toward realizing the dream. When we have something visual to remind us of where we are going, it helps to align our behavior with our dreams.

A vision board can help us to answer internal questions we might have. It can serve as an extension of our creative process or enable us to find clarity in regard to something we have been contemplating. Visual aids engage our brain by helping us to integrate ideas and give them a sense of reality. Adding pictures or other visual media to your board can further enhance your vision board.

A vision board is not a to-do list or a way to plan your life. It may help to have other tools for these purposes, but a vision board is meant to inspire you on a daily basis. A dry-erase board is typically a good choice so you can easily grow and evolve your dreams and vision over time. We have found the larger-size boards are excellent for this purpose. A 4-by-3-foot board is our general recommendation. Use multicolored dry-erase markers so you can be creative with it. Hang your vision board somewhere you can see it easily every day. We have found that when other people see our vision boards, it tends to inspire them as well!

MAXIM 7 – ACTION

Be the change you wish to see in the world...
-Gandhi-

Manifesting Our Dreams

We are constantly shifting into a new physical, spiritual, and emotional state. It's comforting and inspiring to know we can change our lives at any moment for the better. No length of time needs to pass for us to qualify as the person we believe we are. These shifts happen every second of every day; almost instantaneously we are given the same opportunity to repeat it. Take advantage of the gift to evolve in a microsecond. We are awesome! Let's do it again!
My shift takes place; now it's in the past.
-TAC-

Through our discussion in Maxim 6, *Dream Design and Visualization* we started the process of aligning our authentic self with our vision. As we grow and develop, our powerful self emerges as the dominant influence in our daily life. Through this realization, we come to understand that there is more for us in this world. This new self might have different dreams, different goals or even a completely different purpose. Through dreaming and visualizing, we start to create a picture of the intentional life we want to lead.

As we gain clarity surrounding the components of what this life looks like, we need to do more than think about it. It is time to take actionable steps toward manifesting the externals we need to make this life a reality. One of the initial stumbling blocks for most of us is, "Where do we start?" The answer is right now, right here, in this moment.

Dreaming and visualizing are the initial steps of the process. Now we continue by taking tangible steps each and every moment of every day.

Do What's in Front of You

When we want to move toward action, we can get stuck by feeling we need the whole solution in order to move forward. We may feel as if we need to know every step it will take to accomplish our goal or intention. This can lead to fear and anxiety or simply paralysis. We start forming hypothetical scenarios: what might happen if I do "x"? Or, we may feel a sudden desire to wait for the right time.

The reality is, most things are accomplished as a result of a series of small actions and initiatives. The most sophisticated navigation technology flies planes in as direct a line as possible, which in the end is merely thousands of small missteps and recalculations as the plane is bandied about in the air.

When we are confronted with especially large tasks like starting a business, for example, or making a career change, it is often more efficient to break the larger task into smaller tasks. We can begin by prioritizing the things which need to be done first and/or the things we can do right now in our current situation.

It might even make sense when we are really feeling overwhelmed to break things down into a minute-by-minute actionable timetable. Think about what you absolutely must do right now. Many times the answer is, nothing right now in this moment. Taking the time to break down large tasks into smaller pieces helps bring clarity to efficient actions we can take and reduces our anxiety and pre-worrying.

A new beginning can start now! History is happening every millisecond and the only thing that holds on to our past is our mind. That crazy tissue between our ears works very hard to remind us of past experiences and future unknowns. The fact of the matter is that living in this very moment by making the correct decisions is our best approach to a predictable future! Although the future is unpredictable, we have the ability to choose our emotional state and actions in the current space. The outcome: positive results that align with this behavior. What you ask for is what you will get! Just be authentic, present, and aware of the results. Simple – now I have to practice!
Our best opportunity to change our past and future is living in the moment.
-TAC-

There is rarely the perfect time and set of circumstances to start any task. We probably wouldn't even recognize the moment if it appeared. There can certainly be better opportunities than others given the conditions, but most of the time there is something we can do to get things moving in the right direction. Life is a product of momentum. Change is a constant we all deal with in every moment. Our life's direction is defined by our current momentum. If we want to effect change or create something new, we begin with dreaming and visualization. Once we have some clarity in regard to the direction we would like to head, we take small, actionable steps to move our momentum in that direction.

When you have made a conscious and intentional decision to pursue a course of action, use the five-second rule. Within five seconds of any actionable thought, do something to start the momentum. Write down the first step. Take notes on some of the things that need to be done. Put something on your calendar or a Post-it note on the refrigerator or in the cupboard, committing you to action. This helps you to emotionally commit to doing something about your actionable thought and begins to shift the momentum.

The Journey

One day you finally knew
what you had to do, and began,
though the voices around you
kept shouting
their bad advice--
though the whole house
began to tremble
and you felt the old tug
at your ankles.
"Mend my life!"
each voice cried.
But you didn't stop.
You knew what you had to do,
though the wind pried
with its stiff fingers
at the very foundations,
though their melancholy
was terrible.
It was already late
enough, and a wild night,
and the road full of fallen
branches and stones.
But little by little,
as you left their voices behind,
the stars began to burn
through the sheets of clouds,
and there was a new voice
which you slowly
recognized as your own,
that kept you company
as you strode deeper and deeper
into the world,
determined to do
the only thing you could do
determined to save
the only life you could save.
-Mary Oliver-

Patience vs. Procrastination

It is important to know the difference between acting intentionally and unintentionally. Knowing the difference between being patient and procrastinating is crucial to acting in alignment with your core values and beliefs. We've been speaking about taking action quickly to develop momentum, but this is based on having a clear vision of the action we want to take. In some circumstances, if we are not clear about our course of action, or are uncertain about our motive for acting, practicing patience is an important action.

Procrastination, on the other hand, is self-defeating behavior. It is making the choice to engage in a pleasurable activity over delaying gratification. Sometimes it is a reaction to stress and serves as a coping mechanism. The choice to temporarily cave is a poor one, however, with long-term consequences. Procrastination can become a habit. It may be indulged due to fear of failure, self-doubt, or any number of self-defeating patterns of behavior.

Wu Wei – Action without Action

As counter-intuitive as it might sound, sometimes the greatest action we can take is none. By deciding not to take action, we allow things to unfold; we allow new information to manifest itself in that moment. We may even set an action in motion by waiting. It may be that someone else acts and, in fact, demonstrates greater skill than we might have been capable of, or the lack of action allows something which was already in motion, unseen to us, to develop into its full potential.

There is a sense of patience and prudence in non-action. We are, in fact, acting when we choose not to, simply because making a choice is still *acting*. Choosing not to act is an action. It is acting in a patient and sometimes compassionate manner. Maybe we have a friend who could clearly benefit from our help, but by acting on their behalf, we rob them of a valuable experience. Or perhaps we feel compelled to act on a piece of information, but find ourselves hesitant to do so. While we hesitate, new information comes before us which completely alters the course of action we would have chosen previously.

In non-action we find humility as well. Sometimes our desire to act is rooted in our own needs and not the needs of others. We can become self-righteous very easily by feeling as if it is our job to act in every situation. Giving others space to be themselves can be one of our greatest actions. Every parent and teacher has delighted in hesitating and then watching a child grasp an idea on their own.

Act without acting; Serve without concern for affairs; Find flavor in what has no flavor. Regard the small as large and the few as many, and repay resentment with kindness.
Plan for the difficult while it is easy; Act on the large while it is minute.
The most difficult things in the world begin as things that are easy; The largest things in the world arise from the minute. Therefore the Sage, to the end does not strive to be great; Those who too lightly agree will necessarily be trusted by few; And those who regard many things as easy will necessarily end up with many difficulties. Therefore, even the sage regards things as difficult,
And as a result, in the end has no difficulty. [58]
-Lao-Tzu-

Conscious vs. Impulsive Behavior

Conscious action requires presence and clarity. It is action which stems from alignment with our core values and beliefs. It is rooted in self-awareness and a connected awareness of the present situation. Conscious action is not only aligned with our values and beliefs, but with the reality of the situation we are in. If we are truly seeing things as

---

[58] "Lao-Tzu Te-Tao Ching" Henricks, p. 32

they are, we can act accordingly in any given situation. Conscious action is a direct result of engaging our powerful self in our decision-making.

Impulsive behavior is rooted in unconsciousness. It is not always negative behavior as sometimes, impulsive behavior is simply spontaneous and appropriate to the situation we are in. When we do not possess clarity in a given situation, acting impulsively often leads to poor results and negative consequences. The powerless self will typically choose to act impulsively in order to exert a feeling of control. Impulse control comes from discipline and learning to delay gratification. It is a direct result of cultivating patience.

Responding, Not Reacting

When we are present and connected to our lives, it can be said that we begin to respond rather than react to situations. Responding is the ability to maintain your physical, mental and spiritual composure in response to others' actions. When we are faced with an external situation which triggers our emotions, our habitual response is to react. We may get angry or scared and then we react by lashing out, withdrawing or escaping. When we respond, we give ourselves a moment of space to allow the emotional reaction to be felt, then we make a conscious decision as to how we want to engage the situation.

By taking a moment to be present and connected to the situation, we can typically see the situation more objectively and respond appropriately to it. This is the idea of not forcing our will, emotions or desires onto the external. Instead, we can adapt to the external rather than be pushed around by it. We can think of this in terms of our powerful and powerless self. When we find ourselves reacting to situations, especially from a place of fear or anger, it is often the powerless self showing up. When we can connect to a situation, create some space and consciously respond, we will recognize the traits of our powerful self running the show.

Creating space and time for your powerful self is an excellent way to prevent creating new resentments. When we react, we often can feel victimized by the external event. If you learned to stop creating new resentments, you also quickly learn how to empathize with situations from a place of compassion and are able to withhold judgment. This is the gift we give when we respond instead of react. It further allows us to live our life authentically.

Skillful Action

When we take the time and effort to act, we want to be as effective as possible. We may not conceive of a specific outcome or expectation, but as humans we enjoy being productive. We have discussed various concepts of acting, from patience to impulsivity and other barriers to effective action. Bringing all of the positive components of action is a skill we can acquire over time.

A.C.T.I.O.N

*Does this action **A**lign with my values and beliefs?*
*Do I have a **C**lear view of the situation ?*
*Is this the right **T**ime?*
*Am I acting **I**ntentionally?*
*How does this affect **O**thers?*
*Is it **N**ecessary for me to act?*

We strive for the right amount of action in any given moment. We want to maintain a balance between our individual needs in any given moment and the needs of others. We may have a clear picture of taking action which will effectively serve our interests, but what if it comes at the expense of others? Maintaining this balance is a product of being present in the moment. If we are connected to the situation, we can see things more clearly.

If we can put aside our own agenda and ego, we can see the situation *as it is*. This is a state of awareness without expectation or judgment. We are trying to be as objective as possible. We have described suffering as "the gap between expectation and reality." If we can close that gap in any situation, we will find ourselves much closer to the truth.

If we are present and authentic, our powerful self runs the show. We are acting in alignment with our values and beliefs. From this level of awareness we can dance with the situation. Instead of simply controlling or manipulating the situation, we work with the resources that are available to us. We can be mindful of our own purpose while respecting the purpose of everyone and everything. We can pause and determine whether or not it is the appropriate time for us to act or whether it is even necessary for us to act at all. Success breeds further success, and soon positive results are their own natural reward.

Drop Your Story Part II – Take Action!

We don't need to hold back our actions anymore. We have dropped the boundaries and restrictions of our story. We no longer need to seek external validation from others in order to have permission to act. We no longer need to be afraid to fail. We know our actions are born from our powerful, authentic self. When we are living authentically, we no longer need a story to help us identify who we are, or why we belong. Our firm identity begins to serve as a boundary which limits our possibilities.

If we can drop our story completely, we can live without the habits that hold up or justify our actions. We don't need a resume in order to pursue our dreams. We are good enough, because we are here. We are qualified because our intention is an extension of our core values and beliefs. We need not hesitate and wallow in self-doubt. It is not that we hold all the answers, or that we are better than anyone else. We simply know we are willing to take full accountability for our actions.

Becoming Comfortable Being Uncomfortable

In difficult times, it can be easy to see only the challenges we face. To wish we didn't have to go through them in the first place. We can focus on the pain and discomfort instead of the opportunity before us. Moments of adversity provide an opportunity for growth and change. If we embrace them, they can provide the path for future prosperity. We often want things in our lives like more money or an amazing partner to share our lives with. Are we ready? Do we possess physical, mental and spiritual wealth? Are we an amazing partner? It is wonderful to ask for these things to come into our lives, but if we have not prepared ourselves for them, the result may not be what we anticipated. Adversity provides the gift of preparation.
Overcoming adversity is tapping into prosperity.
-TAC-

We are moving forward as a result of the shift to our powerful self. This is the gift to propel you forward; you will not be able to stay at rest anymore, or at least find any comfort in stasis. What a remarkable process: becoming comfortable being uncomfortable. We learn to act once we have clarity, in spite of any perceived or current discomfort. We face our fears or ambiguity by learning to be at peace with not knowing every little detail or every possible outcome.

"An object at rest tends to stay at rest, an object in motion stays in motion."

Overcoming inertia is an important aspect of taking action. Inertia is the resistance we feel to changing our current state. Many of us have experienced the feeling of not wanting to get off the couch when we have already spent half the day on it. The same can be said for behavioral patterns we have fallen into. If we have not been to the gym in weeks or months, we find it increasingly difficult to find the motivation to get started again. However, once we start taking action, we gain momentum and are likely to be motivated to continue.

Many people find it initially harder to engage in vitally absorbing activities, and at first easier to sit on their backsides and do little. When they go on in spite of this difficulty and force themselves into activity, they come to enjoy their

actions more than they enjoy passivity. The game normally is worth the candle - if you keep playing it long enough.[59]

Sometimes we have trouble taking action due to fear. It is more comfortable for us to simply not try than to take the risk of failure. We may say we don't feel like it when we really mean something else. If you find yourself not feeling like doing something you want to do, take some time to reflect on the true reason behind your inaction. If you cannot find a reasonable reason for not acting, such as being physically ill or otherwise incapable, take some time for a self-audit of the underlying reasons.

Complacency is comfortable. As we mentioned before, you don't have to take a risk, you don't have to face any fear, and quite simply, we get used to being complacent. Complacency can very easily become a habit. Human beings naturally gravitate to things they know or are used to doing. Taking action to change your life requires effort and discipline. Even the thought of change can create fear and anxiety.

---

[59] "A Guide To Rational Living" Ellis Harper, p.208

Learning to embrace and manage change is a skill. Much like other skills, managing change becomes palatable through repetition. Consistently challenge yourself to be a person of action. Abandon the habit of inertia and replace complacency with the habit of action.

Life is difficult.
This is a great truth, one of the greatest truths. It is a
great truth because once we truly see this truth, we transcend
it. Once we truly know that life is difficult – once we truly
understand and accept it – then life is no longer difficult.
Because once it is accepted, that fact that life is difficult
no longer matters. [60]
-M. Scott Peck-

Managing Change

We have been visualizing and dreaming and bringing things into our life. We are now taking action and it becomes important to learn how to accept and manage change as an ongoing constant in our lives. Living a life of intention requires effort and persistence. It requires becoming accustomed to constant change. One of the universal truths of life is that nothing in the universe remains static, so change is inevitable; you don't have a choice. When we get tired, however, and grasp for comfort and pleasure, we often resist change. Life feels like a Chinese finger trap: the harder we resist, the tighter it squeezes us.

By going with the change and embracing it, we may be in for an intense ride, but we learn to acquire the necessary skills to enjoy the ride. Sometimes change is welcomed and at other times it is thrust upon us. We decide how we want to label the change and how we choose to react to it. Change is a catalyst to growth and an essential process of life. We can use this process to our advantage as we change our relationships and restructure our beliefs.

We are bringing in new energy and engaging in a new tempo for our lives. We are becoming spiritual athletes. We cannot continue to develop without the opportunities presented to us through change. It takes time to develop our endurance and

---

[60] M. Scott Peck, *The Road Less Traveled* p.15

aptitude for managing change. For many of us, we have been living our lives up to this point from a place of powerlessness. As our powerful self emerges, it is as if we have been dormant and we need to get in shape or shake the rust off. It is the same if we have not been to the gym for a long time. At first we are sore during and after our workouts. Over time, our body becomes accustomed to the new activity and we grow. We become stronger and we gain endurance.

The same transformation occurs mentally and spiritually. We become more comfortable with change and growth. The initial growing pains become growth signals. The discomfort -pain *and* gain - becomes a positive sign that we are headed in the right direction. We start to thrive on change rather than avoid it. We welcome opportunities that put us in a position to grow and develop.

Positive Stress

As we continue to develop the habit of taking action and learn to embrace and manage change, we typically encounter stress. In our society, stress has negative connotations as something to be avoided. There are different types of stress, though, and they are not all bad. The stress we feel when we are going through a traumatic experience is certainly not healthy. It is extremely important to take the time to engage in self-care, to seek out support and heal from this type of stress. We covered this extensively in Maxim 5, *Sustainability*.

The stress we endure by pursuing our passion, by living a life of intention, is entirely different. It is a useful tool to help motivate us and to give us feedback that we are growing and evolving. Positive stress helps us stretch and grow. It expands our capabilities and competence. It can help to provide us with the energy we need to engage in challenging activities. This positive stress increases our levels of dopamine and serotonin, increasing neurotransmitter function. It prepares us to act at a high level.

The way we view stress has an important impact on the effect it has on us. A good example is the stress we feel when we are speaking to a large group. Many people perceive the stress they feel before public speaking as negative. They may say they have a fear of public speaking. If we view the stress we feel before speaking as our body and mind rising to the occasion, we get a much different effect from this stress. The jitters help to focus and welcome the performer or speaker to the task.

Comfort Zone/Stretch Zone/Alive Zone

The stretch zone is a way to transcend our comfort zone. The stretch zone closes the gap between what we have accomplished and the unknown. This helps us expand into new territory beyond our present level of comfort. We want to strike a balance of living at our edge, and just a bit beyond it. The stretch zone promotes living in a consistent state of growth and development, building upon the last step while taking the next one.

> *In any given moment, a man's growth is optimized if he leans just beyond his edge, his capacity, his fear. He should not be too lazy, happily stagnating in the zone of security and comfort. Nor should he push far beyond his edge, stressing himself unnecessarily, unable to metabolize his experience. He should lean just slightly beyond the edge of fear and discomfort. Constantly. In everything he does.*[61]
> **-David Deida-**

The alive zone is where we become accustomed to and thrive on change. We look forward to the opportunity that

---

[61] "The Way of The Superior Man" Deida, p.29

change presents for us and seek out any chance to explore life. We have let go of our perceived boundaries and resist forming new ones.

Values + Beliefs + Actions = Authenticity (revisited)

We don't compromise our values or beliefs, but we remain flexible in how to put them into action. This is the difference between being stubborn and flexible. Our actions are based on these fundamental values and beliefs. If we act from a place of self-righteousness or arrogance, we are missing the point. Our journey of growth and development is not a means to show our superiority over others, or to gain control over the external world. This is a battle we will eventually lose, no matter how powerful we become. Humility is one of our most powerful character traits to help us manage feelings of superiority. One of the most effective strategies is to practice prudence.

Prudence

prudent
1. *discreet or cautious in managing one's activities; circumspect.*
2. *practical and careful in providing for the future.*
3. *exercising good judgment or common sense.*[62]

Prudence helps us to combine wisdom and practicality in our actions. It is a guideline for efficiency in how we choose to allocate our resources in any given moment. We believe in infinite possibilities, yet in any given moment we have a certain amount of energy and resources available to

---

[62] http://dictionary.reference.com/browse/prudent

us. These resources are infinitely available, especially when they are needed.

> *Prudence is the virtue of the senses. It is the science of appearances. It is the outmost action of the inward life. It is God taking thought for oxen. It moves matter after the laws of matter. It is content to seek health of body by complying with physical conditions, and health of mind by the laws of the intellect.*[63]
> *-Ralph Waldo Emerson-*

The Myth of Multi-Tasking

Most people believe they're good at multitasking. They aren't. Modern scientific research is beginning to show evidence as to why human beings are not very good at multitasking. Sure, we can handle a simple automatic activity like walking and talking, but when it comes to managing complex or competing tasks, we are not very good at it.

> *Multitasking involves engaging in two tasks simultaneously. But here's the catch. It's only possible if two conditions are met: 1) at least one of the tasks is so well learned as to be automatic, meaning no focus or thought is necessary to engage in the task (e.g., walking or eating) and 2) they involve different types of brain processing.*[64]

Human beings have intuitively known this for centuries. We understand how powerful it is to focus in and be present with what we are doing. This is why mindfulness practices such as meditation are becoming so popular. They teach us to focus on one thing at a time and give all of our attention to it.

We want to be clear about focusing our energy in our actions. Yes, we want to act in a consistent and effective

---

[63] "Prudence" *Complete works of Emerson,* p.158

[64] http://www.psychologytoday.com/blog/the-power-prime/201103/technology-myth-multitasking

manner, but if our energy is scattered across multiple competing tasks, we are essentially treading water. This is not skillful action, but essentially becomes action for the sake of action; it is akin to simply busying yourself. This is more of a constant doing mode as opposed to *being*. We believe we are getting more done because we are engaged in so many activities at an external level, but how much are we truly accomplishing?

Effective action, as we discussed earlier, is based on presence. We are present with the moment. We are presenting our powerful authentic self in the moment. By focusing, we are able to engage in skillful, prudent action. We are so tuned in we can decide whether it is appropriate to act or not and in what way best suits the totality of the situation. This is *focus*. Focus is the antidote to multi-tasking and distraction. The more we practice focusing our mind and body toward our actions, the more effective and efficient we become.

Plan of Action

How do we develop a plan of action? What are the key components? How do the currently available resources fit? We need a set of short-, mid- and long-term actionable items in order to move forward toward our intention. By taking the time to think through and write down our plan, we create momentum toward our goal and begin to manifest our vision. Writing out our plan of action is the first step of the process in making a commitment to ourselves.

It's best to start with a 30-day plan that involves doing the things that are currently available and accessible to you. It could be as simple as doing some research or making contact with people who may be able to help. It might include making a few behavioral changes. Sometimes it involves simply organizing and preparing to take action. Ideally, we want the first part of our plan to be easily accomplished so we can gain confidence in our ability to follow through.

Our mid-term goals may be anywhere from the 30- to 120-day window of our plan. This is when we plan to get into the active part of the process. We are beginning to see some results from our early efforts and are starting to make progress on the bulk of the work required to bring our dreams to fruition. Here we are setting the groundwork for the entire process and making headway toward gathering other resources we may need to complete the project.

Long-term goals may be anywhere from six months to a year or beyond. This is usually part of a plan of action which involves longer-term life changes, like a new career or buying a home or starting a business. This helps us to place our intention on persevering through the process and not losing faith as obstacles present themselves. When we write out a longer-term plan we are committing ourselves internally to seeing things through.

No plan of action is meant to be restrictive. We create a plan to give us a starting point and to help guide us and motivate us to follow through. Many things we cannot anticipate will come up along the way and we adjust accordingly when they do. In fact, we may not want to be too specific in our planning unless it is absolutely necessary. The plan of action is simply a way for us to materialize our dreaming and visualizing. Leave room to be surprised, as not all unforeseen events are unfavorable. Many may speed you along or help you open up to even greater possibilities!

Exercise: The Alive Zone (TAZ)

4 Circles:
1. *Center Circle* – Comfort Zone
2. *Second Ring* – Stretch Zone
3. *Third Ring* – Dead Zone
4. *Fourth Ring* – Alive Zone

Comfort Zone – Current state without change that feels safe.

Stretch Zone – Minute-by-minute decisions and defined actions which push our boundaries. We choose manageable but challenging achievements to expand the stretch zone.

Dead Zone – Space of doubt, fear, distraction, limiting beliefs, lack of experience, and deception.

Alive Zone – Complete belief in the vision, results, and passionate connection to the outcome.

1. In order to move outside of our comfort zone, we find manageable actions, or steps, setting our vision into motion through action. Through the process of trial and error, we shift closer to our goals.

Example: Writing a book. To think of a completed book may scare us away from taking action, but we can start by:
- Purchasing a pen and journal.
- Freestyling and writing your first sentence.
- Developing a pattern of writing.
- Completing a page, then two, then three, etc....
- Downloading to a workable computer format.
- Sending out to edit.
- Sharing completed edited version.
- Researching publishing options.

- Procuring the designated funding.
- Publishing, presenting, and selling.

2. In the stretch zone we perform the actions in front of us without hesitation. We will begin to engage actionable steps and build momentum toward our goals.

3. By recognizing limiting thoughts and distractions, we place them in the dead zone. We realize these are merely perceptions and do not need to dictate our behavior. We have not accomplished the vision, so it is impossible for us to compare it to past results. New adventures and experiences don't have a point of reference in our memory or history.

4. Dream the end result and allow yourself to live in the space of accomplishment and outcome. Smell it, feel it, see it, hear it and taste it. Emotionally attach yourself to the physical space of accomplishing your desired result. Describe and feel the result as if you have already completed all of the required actions on the journey. Celebrate your accomplishment and express your gratitude for the process. Believe how amazing you are by overcoming your fear and tapping into your perseverance. You are AWESOME!!! This is what the alive zone feels like!

The result of living in the moment, managing the minute-by-minute decisions and doing what is in front of you is experiencing you (the alive zone). We do not have fear of our current space. The only time we experience fear is when we are projecting and anticipating the dead zone. The dead zone will diminish as we develop and expand our stretch zone. Soon our comfort zone will be our alive zone!

Tool: *Get*-To-Do List

Most of us have some kind of to-do list at all times. It often consists of various items we need to accomplish, like household or work-related tasks. These help us to remember the things we need to do as part of our general commitments, but they are not often things that inspire us.

A *get*-to-do list gives us a reminder of how grateful and passionate our life really is. It helps us to see beyond our mundane daily tasks and opens us up to the many things we *get* to do which enrich our lives and the lives of those around us. We can use a *get*-to-do list to help us shift our perspective on tasks we might take for granted or find unpleasant. We might think doing work around our home is a chore, but we can also consider how fortunate we are to have a home to work on in the first place!

Get-to-do lists might include:
1. Tasks
2. Bucket list items
3. Things we might have been putting off
4. Small, actionable steps toward goals
5. Personal items
6. Relationships
7. Career

Maxim 8 – Being of Service

From the moment we begin our life in this world, the universe is
aligned. The fact that we have clean, air, water, and nutrients to fuel
our bodies is amazing. We were all born with the ability to love, feel
loved, share compassion and seek happiness. We all have the same stuff
and it's incredible to think about how epic this reality is. Sometimes
life presents us with challenges but this builds our character. Say hello
to people…hold open the door…let the car sneak in front of you…tell
people you love them and believe it.
We are a miracle.
-TAC-

Love

*"When you love you wish to do things for. You wish to
sacrifice for. You wish to serve."*
-Ernest Hemingway-
A Farewell to Arms

Love yourself first and always. We cannot love others
wholeheartedly without love of self. We deserve love and
kindness just as much as anyone else in this world. Even
when we are not at our best, we are still deserving of love.
Love is inclusive. Just like our practice of self-compassion,
we must practice self-love in order to be able to share this
love with others. Without our being in love with ourselves,
we cannot share our love with the world and everything in
it. The love of others is restricted only by the capacity for
inner love.

Love After Love

The time will come
when, with elation
you will greet yourself arriving
at your own door, in your own mirror
and each will smile at the other's welcome,
and say, sit here. Eat.
You will love again the stranger who was your self.
Give wine. Give bread. Give back your heart
to itself, to the stranger who has loved you
all your life, whom you ignored
for another, who knows you by heart.
Take down the love letters from the bookshelf,
the photographs, the desperate notes,
peel your own image from the mirror.
Sit. Feast on your life.
-Derek Walcott-

Giving and receiving love are equally important. Much like compassion, love grows when we give it away. When we turn our intention toward sharing it with others, we grow in our capacity to love. This inner-outer, outer-inner relationship is reciprocal. They feed off of each other in an ever-expanding relationship.

Reciprocation of love doesn't always come in the same form we share it. Keep an open mind because the delivery may look different but still have an equal meaning behind it. We are all unique and express ourselves in our own way. Don't deny yourself the love in front of you because of your perception of love. Love without limits and celebrate the efforts of others.
You don't need to be loved the same way you love.
-TAC-

Unconditional Love

Love gives naught but itself and takes naught but from itself. Love possesses not nor would it be possessed; For love is sufficient unto love.[65]
-Kahlil Gibran-

The greatest love we aspire to as humans is unconditional. This is love without judgment, without expectation, without attachment of any kind. We love for the sake of loving itself. Our ability to love unconditionally grows from our ability to grow and develop toward a state of self-actualization.

Maslow explicitly defines self-actualization as "the desire for self-fulfillment, namely the tendency for him [the individual] to become actualized in what he is potentially. This tendency might be phrased as the desire to become more and more what one is, to become everything that one is capable of becoming.[66]

As humans, we aspire to reach our full potential. We desire the freedom and resources to present our authentic self to the world. This aspiration contains components of our soul purpose...our unique gift...our mission. We may easily say all of these things are driven by and contain love. Love may be the best word we have to describe the passion and feeling we have inside to be of service to the world. Unconditional love is its highest form.

---

[65] "The Prophet" Gibran, p.12
[66] http://en.wikipedia.org/wiki/Self-actualization-Maslow.27s_characteristics_of_self-actualizers

Power of Example

We can do so many things to improve the environment and the world we live in. One way we can be of service and help others in need is to set an example of lifestyle. During times of struggle, challenge, and despair, we often want to offer some form of assistance. The best way we can be of service is to work on ourselves and exemplify strong character. We are all contributors and agents of change.
Being a power of example is free.
-TAC-

It can be difficult to act selflessly and without expectation. Our desire to be acknowledged or appreciated can be very strong, especially when we don't feel powerful. When we have grown enough to transcend the need for external validation, we open ourselves up to be of service without expectation. We feel gratified by simply contributing to the world in any way we can. We act because we want to, not because we have to or because we feel the burden of expectation from others. We are simply being ourselves in the world.

Example is not the main *thing in influencing others. It is the* only *thing. Hope is renewed each time that you see a person you know, who is deeply involved in the struggle of life, helping another person. You are the unaffected witness and must agree that there is hope for mankind.*
-Albert Schweitzer-
Thoughts for Our Times

One of the most powerful gifts we give in being ourselves is the power of example. When we see others suffering, we might feel the desire to step in and do something. Sometimes this is a wise choice. Other times, by simply being present and setting an example, we can be more helpful. Giving advice or helping someone out is a good solution, but the more powerful we become, the greater our impact is in simply being. By relating authentically to others, we create a deeper connection. Sometimes our presence goes beyond even our words and actions.

Power Is Connection

If we could have an unconditional relationship with even one person, we could have an unconditional relationship with the world.
-Pema Chodron-

No one exists uniquely in this universe. Nothing exists in complete separation from everything else. The universe is a vast web of connection. Even outer space is filled with dark matter and other yet-to-be-discovered energy. Science and spiritual traditions converge on this concept unanimously. We might want to believe, for our own selfish reasons, that we exist as a separate entity from our environment. This is often true when we do not want to accept the responsibility of our actions or to be affected by the actions of others. This illusion can only be supported by the ego. It is indeed an illusion.

The enlightened philosophers of the seventeenth century, including Rene Descartes, were champions of the individual as a unique and exclusively important entity. This gave rise to the rights of the individual within democracy, which was wonderful. However, there have been erroneous assumptions which have permeated Western culture since.

I think, therefore I am.
-Rene Descartes-

This one sentence has had a profound impact on egocentric thinking. The idea that our consciousness alone qualifies us as being separate from the world gave rise to individualism, with its notion of the importance of self over others. This has perpetuated a culture of self-importance, which has led to much suffering in our world.

The loneliness and disconnection that is inherent in this way of thinking is devastating to our sense of purpose and belonging. It allows us to live under the illusion that we are not affected by the suffering of others, that we do not share in the joy and success of others, and that we are ultimately alone in this life. However beguiling, this illusion could not be further from the truth.

> *To sustain ourselves, we need balance. The challenge comes when we are not feeling our best, which often leads us to neglect the things we need to do to get back on track. These moments create a cycle of stagnation and it can feel like we are treading water through life. How do we break these cycles without a sheer act of will? We can only tread water for so long; the support of others becomes crucial. We do need to accept responsibility for our own health and wellbeing, but we can accept the help of others when it is needed. We do not need to make things difficult on purpose. An unwillingness to accept help when it is offered is more a sign of weakness than needing the help in the first place.*
> **Be of and accept service when the opportunity arises.**
> **-TAC-**

Connection is the ultimate power of humanity. Our ability to connect and empathize with one another is a great resource we all depend on in every moment. It allows us to engage in the richness of life. We all benefit from each other's contributions, and we all suffer together.

Being of Service to Yourself

Much like love and compassion, service starts with self. If we care for ourselves, we are caring for everyone and everything in our lives. By presenting the best version of ourselves to the world, we live in a state of constant service to others. The commitment we make to growth and development benefits everyone we come into contact with. The example we set, the love we give and the compassion we have is an extension of being of service to ourselves. Taking care of our own house and being is not self-centeredness – it is self-awareness and self-actualization. Self-centeredness is egocentric; self-awareness is ego-transcendence.

Being of Service to Others

It seems foreign to many, to simply give without expectation of reward. When we realize the reward is in the act of giving itself, we begin to truly find ourselves in everyone and everything around us. When we let go of the result, we can act simply from an authentic place. If we have grown beyond self-importance, we begin to see how being of service to others is being of service to self. We don't need the recognition, the validation or the external reward. We live a life of service because it is the true expression of who we are.

Competition vs. Cooperation

"Competition has been shown to be useful up to a certain point and no further, but cooperation, which is the thing we must strive for today, begins where competition leaves off."
-Franklin D. Roosevelt-
Speech at the People's Forum in Troy, New York (March 3, 1912)

Competition is outdated and inefficient. It has served its purpose over the course of human evolution, but the next phase of human development will be built around cooperation. As human beings have evolved from our animal origins, we have continued to develop as conscious beings. Competition can drive development and improvement, but it is far less efficient than cooperation. In cooperative environments, human beings benefit from the work of one another rather than benefitting at someone else's expense.

The dualistic thinking of our society is marked by competition: winners and losers, right and wrong, black and white. We know intuitively that these concepts impose unacceptable limits. They are attractive because they allow our powerless selves to make sense of an uncertain world. They indulge the darker sides of human desire: greed, envy, and lust. They feel safe on the surface because they make an unpredictable world predictable, yet we all suffer in this illusion of certitude. It robs us of our freedom and our uniqueness.

Cooperation is expansive and inclusive. Cooperation creates space for engagement and involvement. It requires powerful people and it supports the development of powerful people. Cooperation expands the resources available to us. Conversely, competition revolves around a fixed pie in which the participants compete for the pieces. In cooperative environments, we can strive for improvement through expansion and to the benefit of the group. We may not always achieve such a desirable outcome, but it is certainly worth the effort.

Letting Go of Judgment

When we see ourselves as separate or disconnected from the world, we easily fall into judgment. Our powerless self feels shame and loneliness, so we lash out at others in an attempt to regain control. When we judge others, we inherently judge ourselves. We create a comparison between self and other under the illusion of separateness. Judgment is a product of the inner and outer critic. It is often engaged when we feel hurt or powerless.

> *Letting go and getting out of our own way is a liberating experience. By offering ourselves to others with no concern for ridicule, we are an example of authenticity. Don't be afraid of what others will think or say, just be true to yourself. It is so comforting to be free of preconceived notions of how others perceive your values. There is no judgment here, only support of your organic self! If you give it all away, there is nothing which can be taken.*
> **In ultimate vulnerability lies ultimate strength.**
> **-TAC-**

Humility

In our commitment to living a life of service, humility is key. Humility helps us to temper our ego when we feel rejected or unrewarded. Humility helps to cut down any sense of entitlement or superiority when we give to the world. Humility grounds us in authenticity. Without humility, our service can foster feelings of self-righteousness. Our desire to live authentically deepens our connection to the world. Pride, on the other hand, strengthens our ego and self-importance, our weaker self.

Finding, developing and engaging our powerful self in each moment is not for the purpose of proving to the world how great we are or how much more powerful we are. Being of service is not our way of showing the world how compassionate we can be so everyone can praise us. We live this way because it is who we are. It is natural and it is an extension of the love and compassion we hold in our hearts. Without humility, this is simply another way for us to measure our progress against an external standard. No one keeps score; there are no winners or losers competing in a life of service, only more (or less) service.

Equanimity

> *Equanimity is one of the most sublime emotions of Buddhist practice. It is the ground for wisdom and freedom and the protector of compassion and love. While some may think of equanimity as dry neutrality or cool aloofness, mature equanimity produces a radiance and warmth of being. The Buddha describes a mind filled with equanimity as "abundant, exalted, immeasurable, without hostility and without ill-will.*[67]

True service is not discriminatory or exclusive. We don't decide one person or group is more deserving of our service than another. We may determine our specific contribution is better used in one place over another, but we make the decision from a place of compassion and non-judgment. We don't do so based on judgment or bias or whom we think deserves it more. We strive to be of service at all times, in every moment – not just to the people we like or agree with or our immediate neighbors or co-workers, but to everyone and everything.

Universal Compassion

Our capacity to be of service is a product of our cultivation of love. Our ability to connect with others and empathize is born from compassion. As we grow and evolve, we connect to the world at a deeper level. Without compassion, it is easy for us to fall into judgment and

---

[67]http://www.insightmeditationcenter.org/books-articles/articles/equanimity/

disconnection. When we see undesirable qualities in others, we shame them or exclude them. In doing so, we exclude ourselves and the cycle continues.

Compassion is the antidote to anger and resentment. It is also a rich component of service. Compassion motivates us to connect and to cultivate not only ourselves but the world around us. It joins us to the "other" parts of the world and helps us to accept and embrace things exactly as they are, right now, in this moment, without wishing for or desiring things to be anything else.

Cultivate Joy

Through our discussion of service, we can almost feel as if service is simply selfless sacrifice. Yes, at times, we may put others' wellbeing ahead of our own, but when we do so it is because it serves us at a higher level. We do so because the experience is gratifying and therefore joyful. Living authentically is embracing a life of gratifying experience over merely seeking pleasure. It is the enduring joy we feel from living this way which sustains our desire to continue. It grants us a deeper sense of satisfaction and fulfillment in our life.

We love joyfully when we live in alignment with our core values and beliefs...when we act according to these beliefs in conjunction with our personal mission or soul purpose. Living authentically, intentionally and from a place of power, we derive great joy from every moment of our lives. We see even those moments which may cause pain or suffering as integral to the whole of our existence. There is opportunity in all of it.

Daily Actions – Spiritual – Listen, Play, Serve

We all want to be heard, recognized, and acknowledged, but do we provide this support for others? Becoming connected to everyone we come into contact with starts with listening. This gives others an opportunity to be heard. We can learn so much more when we tune in to the communication rather than waiting to speak and/or thinking about what we are going to say next. Mindfulness is becoming connected to each moment by paying attention to what is right in front of you, not thinking about what has been said before or what might be said in the future. We sometimes have little faith in ourselves and this can lead to overthinking our responses as opposed to taking in the information being presented to us. When we connect authentically to the person we are communicating with, we can then respond from a place of authenticity.
-TAC-

1. *Listen* – A simple concept, but do we do this throughout our day, or do we merely listen to our own internal voice? Listening is one of the fundamental ways in which we can connect with others. Simply listening while engaging one another in conversation presents a chance to truly hear the other. How about our environment? The earth creates a beautiful symphony every day, in every hour and season, if only we care to stop and listen to it. Even the hum of a large city has its own beauty. Listening allows us to absorb our environment and truly connect with it.

2. *Play* – Yes, go out and play! As adults we can lose this inherent desire to simply explore and interact with our environment. We are inundated with thoughts of our future, work, and other "serious" concepts. Returning to a childlike state helps us to

remember the joy of curiosity and discovery. Take some time to engage children or animals. Go outside and explore the outdoors. Look at the plants and wildlife. Engage in sports or other active pursuits that make you laugh and smile. Explore your creative nature. Play music, draw, paint – do anything which helps you explore beauty and creativity.

3. *Serve* – Be of service on a daily basis. Offer a kind gesture, a compliment or a favor for a friend or a stranger. This is the exercise of the soul. Share yourself with the world around you. Being of service helps us to connect with the "we" instead of retreating to a state of "I." Cooperation is one of humanity's most desirable traits. Taking time to be of service exercises our spirit and helps us to cultivate our spiritual nature.

The Journey Is Your Reward
Our new religion shouts
What the voices of old religions
Have whispered to our souls
Since the beginning of time:
Our pursuit of pleasure is costly.
It is born of the suffering of others.
Unleash relentlessness for precious gifts
Gratitude
Service
Unconditional love
Do not waltz blindly to the end.
Open your eyes to the present
The journey is your reward.
-TAC-

Everything is part of the path. Our goal is to learn to navigate our human life with authenticity. We do not "arrive" anywhere. There is no final destination. We are learning to live our lives as they are, in every moment. To arrive in this moment and abandon any desire to reach a specific point. We are learning to let our lives unfold and to unfold with it, without resistance. As we grow and develop, we require less certainty; we learn to be comfortable being uncomfortable. We learn to appreciate and embrace the ambiguity of our existence. We cherish the uncertainty that makes life great.

We engage the journey alone, without an agenda or motive. This state of self-awareness hints at self-actualization. Seeing the world with total clarity, connectedness and presence. Knowing this journey started long before our birth and will continue long after. We are a continuation of life's journey – one that has been unfolding since the beginning of time, maybe even before, and will continue long after our precious human life has ended.

Exercise: Love and Appreciation Notes

In today's world, with so many opportunities to communicate through email, social networks, cell phones, and text messaging, we can forget about the power of a personal handwritten note. Receiving a message from someone who has taken the time to share their LOVE with you is one of the greatest gifts we can offer. The cost is low, but the value is high. It does not have to be long, although it can be. It is the act of reaching out with a personal touch that matters. Once completed, mail the letter, card or note to the recipient.

1) Write yourself a letter identifying all of your great qualities. Share with yourself everything you believe you are and can be. Stay positive and supportive, because in this letter you are the object of the LOVE you share for yourself. No negative or past tense emotions, only pure compassion as if you are caring for the most important person in your life. You are ALIVE, and caring for yourself is the foundation of truly being of service to others.

2) Write a letter to the ones you LOVE the most. Describe the wonderful stories and times you have shared together that made you laugh or inspired you. Express your gratitude for their support and how perfect they are in this world. Let your heart flow in a way that will bring them joy as they hear your true admiration and respect for them. Be authentic, kind, and compassionate.

3) Send "thank you" or "I appreciate you" cards to people. You might choose someone you respect or care for, someone who may least expect this from you. An old boss, a new boss, a leader, a friend, family, someone you met on a plane, a business associate, a teammate. Express some form of admiration, positive feedback and appreciation.

4) Reward an organization, business, or entity with your positive experience. Share your support and honest appreciation for their services, initiative, or mission.

Tool: We Pay It Forward

When we are living a life of service, we begin to lose the distinction between self and other. By engaging in acts of kindness on a daily basis, we understand we are being of service to ourselves and others without boundaries. It might be as simple as providing support for someone through listening without judgment, or a small gift such as picking up a cup of coffee for a coworker without them asking for it. Any token of appreciation is a gift to the giver and the receiver.

Giving without any expectation of reward is an act of humility and unconditional support. When we "pay it forward," we share our experience, strength and hope. This helps us develop greater empathy, compassion and intimacy with the world. Through the practice of selfless giving, we open our hearts to the world and inspire others to do the same.

We hope the G8way has helped you realize how special you are and how connected we all are in this life. We love and appreciate your support and being a part of the G8way. If you have benefitted from reading this book and would like to participate further please visit us at:

www.thealivecommunity.com/g8way

The Alive Community
The Alive Community does not reject anyone or anything
The Alive Community does not pass judgment
The Alive Community does not have any boundaries
The Alive Community accepts everyone as they are
The Alive Community is not "right" or "wrong"
The Alive Community is not exclusive
The Alive Community is cooperative
The Alive Community is inclusive
The Alive Community supports all of us

The Alive Community (TAC) has a vision: to connect you to a global community which supports physical, mental and spiritual health. TAC brings together not only people like you, but values and beliefs for mutual support. By incorporating elements of environment, daily living, community and sustainability, TAC provides support anytime, anywhere.

TAC supports the core consciousness that exists within all of us. It is our mission to rediscover and to reconnect you to this fundamental connection that exists among us. TAC represents the compassion and fundamental goodness within all of us. You are now a part of TAC and we hope to see you soon!

Made in the USA
Charleston, SC
03 April 2015